THE ETHNOMETHODOLOGISTS

KEY SOCIOLOGISTS
Editor: Peter Hamilton
The Open University

KEY SOCIOLOGISTS

Series Editor: PETER HAMILTON

The Open University, Milton Keynes

This series will present concise and readable texts covering the work, life and influence of many of the most important sociologists, and sociologically-relevant thinkers, from the birth of the discipline to the present day. Aimed primarily at the undergraduate, the books will also be useful to pre-university students and others who are interested in the main ideas of sociology's major thinkers.

MARX AND MARXISM

PETER WORSLEY, Professor of Sociology, University of Manchester

MAX WEBER

FRANK PARKIN, Tutor in Politics and Fellow of Magdalen College, Oxford

EMILE DURKHEIM

KENNETH THOMPSON, Reader in Sociology, Faculty of Social Sciences, The Open University, Milton Keynes

TALCOTT PARSONS

PETER HAMILTON, The Open University, Milton Keynes

SIGMUND FREUD

ROBERT BOCOCK, The Open University, Milton Keynes

C. WRIGHT MILLS

J. E. T. ELDRIDGE, Department of Sociology, University of Glasgow

THE FRANKFURT SCHOOL

TOM BOTTOMORE, Professor of Sociology, University of Sussex

GEORG SIMMEL

DAVID FRISBY, Department of Sociology, The University, Glasgow

KARL MANNHEIM

DAVID KETTLER, Professor of Political Studies, Trent University, Ontario, Canada; VOLKER MEJA, Associate Professor of Sociology, Memorial University of Newfoundland, and NICO STEHR, Professor of Sociology, University of Alberta

MICHEL FOUCAULT

BARRY SMART, Department of Sociological Studies, University of Sheffield

THE ETHNOMETHODOLOGISTS

WES SHARROCK and BOB ANDERSON, Department of Sociology, University of Manchester

THE ETHNOMETHODOLOGISTS

WES SHARROCK
and
BOB ANDERSON
Department of Sociology, University of Manchester

ELLIS HORWOOD LIMITED
Publishers · Chichester

TAVISTOCK PUBLICATIONS
London and New York

First published in 1986 by
ELLIS HORWOOD LIMITED
Market Cross House, Cooper Street,
Chichester, Sussex, PO19 1EB, England
and

TAVISTOCK PUBLICATIONS LIMITED
11 New Fetter Lane, London EC4 4EE

Published in the USA by
TAVISTOCK PUBLICATIONS
and ELLIS HORWOOD LIMITED
in association with METHUEN INC.
733 Third Avenue, New York, NY 10017

British Library Cataloguing in Publication Data
Sharrock, Wes
The enthnomethodologists. — (Key sociologists)
1. Ethnomethodology
I. Title II. Anderson, Bob, *1946-* III. Series
301 HM24
ISBN 0–85312–911–8 (Ellis Horwood Limited — Library Edn.)
ISBN 0–85312–949–5 (Ellis Horwood Limited — Student Edn.)
Typeset in Times by Ellis Horwood Limited
Printed in Great Britain by R.J. Acford, Chichester

Table of Contents

Wes Sharrock is Senior Lecturer in Sociology at the University of Manchester. His principal publications are shown below.

Bob Anderson is Senior Lecturer in Sociology at Manchester Polytechnic. With Wes Sharrock he has been at the forefront of British studies of Ethnomethodology, contributing to numerous journals and symposia. He is the co-author of *The Sociology Game* and *The Human Sciences and Philosophy* (with Wes Sharrock and John Hughes). He edited *Applied Perspectives in Sociology* with Wes Sharrock.

Editor's Foreword

Few theoretical positions within modern sociology can have evoked the controversy and incomprehension that ethnomethodology produced, from its first appearance in the mid 1960s, through to the present day. In a discipline where political overtones are frequently the cause of dispute about methodological presuppositions, ethnomethodology is attacked more for its conceptual stance *vis-à-vis* the activity of social research. Far from being politically radical, ethnomethodology is radical in quite a different sense, one which has significance for the whole sociological enterprise. For it is concerned with the possibility of sociological inquiry, with questioning and clarifying how it is possible to make the assumption that a sociology of human social relationships and structures can be developed.

It is in questioning the conceptual and methodological bases of sociological thinking that the true radicalism of ethnomethodology becomes apparent. This can be illustrated by reference to an experience of which anyone who has studied sociology at all seriously will be aware. On coming to sociology for the first time, the student is likely to find it difficult to understand just what it is that the sociologist studies. Some of it appears to be obvious, banal, ordinary—and hence difficult to see why the study was undertaken in the first place, for it is so obviously concerned with what everyone knows. On the other hand, some of sociology seems to deal with levels of abstraction from social experience which are apparently unwarrantable. These latter are often so difficult to understand for the beginning student that he or she thinks the problem is primarily one of comprehending a technical jargon of arcane complexity. The assumption is frequently made that the problem of grasping the sociological enterprise is thus of a purely technical nature. Learning the technical jargon will hence provide access to the meaning of sociology, it would seem. But it soon becomes clear that acquisition of the jargon alone is not the avenue to comprehension. What is required is a change of mental perspective—a sort of gestalt-switch from a taken-for-granted perspective on social reality to one which views that reality as organized, structured and presented in a particular way. Connecting the study of what everyone knows with the theoretical imaging of social reality within the new perspective makes everything slot into place. The enterprise of sociological thinking about the world hence becomes justifiable and acceptable, once the gestalt-switch has been effected, from taken-for-granted to theoretically-informed perspective.

The originality and radicalism of ethnomethodology derives precisely from its concern with the nature of the gestalt-switch which is necessary to think sociologically about human relationships and their organization. The ethnomethodologists believe that the key to understanding social structure is contained within the process of converting taken-for-granted understandings of the social into their theoretical derivations. Such a concern is clearly not fundamentally different from that of other sociological perspectives. However, the *project* of ethnomethodology is distinctively different in the methods it chooses to operationalize social theory—for it is in the area of operationalization itself that the ethnomethodologists have been most critical of conventional sociology, and most innovative in their thinking.

The originality of ethnomethodology and of its principal figures—Garfinkel, Sacks, Cicourel—derives then from its preoccupation with what conventional sociology would call methodological issues. But this would be to make them sound too technical. For the main interest of the approach for conventional sociology is arguably its presentation of foundational matters central to a sociological picture of the world. That the importance of this concern has been lost or misconstrued probably accounts for the controversy which surrounds the approach. But it is also due in part to the milieu and mode of presentation of ethnomethodology. The West Coast image of the approach, the relative lack of publications emanating from the somewhat cult-like and secretive group of central figures within the research tradition, an the apparently bizarre range of techniques used to expose the foundational concerns of ethnomethodology, have all contributed to a gulf between it and conventional sociology.

Wes Sharrock and Bob Anderson have worked for many years within the ethnomethodological research tradition. Their text makes clear why the concerns of this approach continue to be central to the sociological enterprise, and provides a helpful and illuminating discussion of ethno-methodologys main theoretical elements. They ably demonstrate why the ethnomethodologists deserve to figure amongst the Key Sociologists of modern sociology. For despite the relatively small published output of ethnomethodological sociologists, their studies constitute a focused and coherent approach to a distinctive range of problems. It is regrettable that there remains a certain lack of understanding of the ethnomethodological project—and the limited availability of the standard works is perhaps one reason for this. But the present work will serve as an excellent introduction to this literature, and as a base from which to explore further in the area.

Peter Hamilton

Preface

Ethnomethodolgy is an approach to sociology that prides itself on anchoring its thinking in its studies, and tying the studies to materials, declining to discuss principled or programmatic matters in an abstract way and in isolation from the research work in hand, and yet our account of it gives only limited attention to those studies and attends much more to the general issues. This is because we are trying to make a case for looking at ethnomethodology's studies and to give some guidance as to how they might initially be approached. To do this we have to sacrifice the description of the studies in favour of trying to bring out the motivation for them. It is no use standing on the principle that people should understand ethnomethodology through its studies if, after they have looked at those studies, they are going to be no wiser than before. Instead of aiming to describe what has been done in ethnomethodology, then, we have aimed to give some sense of what is going on there, showing, especially, why studies are given such primacy and what role they play. It is only after these things are understood that the studies themselves become substantially more comprehensible. This account does not even begin to substitute for reading the studies themselves, though it should be of assistance in finding a way into them.

We have constructed a line of argument, designed to show how ethnomethodology's practices follow from a set of initial assumptions. We have tried, throughout, to combat the impression that it is an arbitrary, erratic and incoherent exercise by showing the very opposite to be the case.

It is perhaps true that there are difficulties in appreciating the consistency of the main lines in ethnomethodologys thought because of its problematical publishing history, which means that even today there are important documents (such as Harold Garfinkel's doctoral thesis and Harvey Sacks's transcribed lectures) which are virtually unknown. We do not, we should add, think that the difficulty in obtaining this literature provides an adequate excuse for many of the misunderstandings about ethnomethodology that are in circulation. Still, it is not easy to appreciate that the assortment of seemingly disparate pieces making up Garfinkel's *Studies in Ethnomethodology* are the product of some of the most systematic thinking that sociology has seen.

We acknowledge that ethnomethodology does appear very strange to sociologists and that it is quite unconventional in its attitudes and aims, but we have not sought to apologize for this or explain it away. Ethnomethodology does not perhaps differ from other sociologies in the ways it is usually imagined to, but it does set itself apart from them and is rather drastically different from them. The seeming oddity of ethnomethodology, when viewed from the standpoint of other sociologies, is not the product of looking from a rational standpoint at something that is irrational and bizarre but, we suggest, the result of looking from an accepted, taken-for-granted position at something which is new and unfamiliar. We take it as axiomatic that if you start out in different places and go in very different directions, they you will come out in different places too, and that this is just what happens with ethnomethodology and other sociologies. The fact that the things ethnomethodology does do not look like those which normally comprise sociological studies should not count one way or another toward their acceptability. They are not meant to respect the established standards of what is acceptably sociological: if they do conform to these, that is fine, but if they do not then this does not necessarily matter. The questions we ask are (1) do the terms in which ethnomethodology sets up its project make sense and (2), if (1) is accepted, do the things it does make sense *in terms of that project*? Both questions can be answered affirmatively.

Our account is a minimal one. We take only a few main points from ethnomethodology's thinking and give an outline of the points and some of their implications. We have attempted little more than exposition, trying to make the ideas clear and intelligible so that a reader might get the gist of some main tendencies in ethnomethodology, though he or she may still be left feeling that an awful lot more would have to be said to make the arguments convincing. However, we have not been trying to make a case for ethnomethodology as against other kinds of sociology, since our main effort is devoted to giving some impression of what the differences between them are. We are as well aware as anyone that at every point there is much,

much more to be said and that all the remarks we make about what conventional sociologists think, assume, say and do would in a longer discussion require and deserve documentation, elaboration, qualification etc. Overall, we have put the issues as sharply and baldly as we can in order that we may give as uncomplicated an outline of a complicated situation as is possible.

In our first chapter, we say something about the derivation of ethnomethodology from phenomenological philosophy. This is not, however, to establish that ethnomethodology is a species of phenomenological sociology since it is not. The phenomenological background, though, does give some idea as to why ethnomethodology takes the directions that it does.

The second chapter shows how the phenomenological influence leads to a focus of attention on the process of theorizing and, in this case, on the problems of operationalizing sociological theory.

Chapter 3 shows how Harold Garfinkel generated his own project, ethnomethodology, in reponse to the problems of operationalizing social theory by rethinking the theories of Talcott Parsons in the terms provided by Alfred Schutz.

Chapter 4 examines how this project recasts the problematic and strategy of sociological inquiry and follows through, in Chapter 5, to the way in which this recasting motivates inquiries into the organization of ordinary conversation, and, in Chapter 6, into how it would restructure the character of studies of work, using scientific work as the leading example.

The last chapter surveys the main points of controversy that have surrounded ethnomethodology and argues that critics have missed the point and missed their target. The controversy over ethnomethodology may be over, but the argument has yet to begin.

We thank Peter Hamilton, John Hughes and John Lee for comments. We continue to be grateful to all those ethnomethodologists who have given us so much to read and think about. We are especially indebted to the deep and wholly original work of Harold Garfinkel and the late Harvey Sacks.

1

Phenomenological Attitudes

We are in some danger of being seen as writing about yesterday's fad. In the latter half of the 1960s and the early 1970s ethnomethodology make a big impact on sociology worldwide, but that impact was not long-lasting and since that time ethnomethodology has had only a marginal position, given its place in the recounting of the variety of views about sociology but otherwise disregarded. The 1960s saw both the rapid expansion of sociology's institutional base, in the form of university jobs and students, and the development of an acute crisis of identity. If in the 1950s sociology, at least in the USA, had been establishing itself as a respectable discipline and sober profession that would stand comparison with medicine and law (which is what its leading figures hoped) then in the 1960s this was widely rejected in favour of a view of sociology as a radical discipline. There were strong attacks on the more entrenched sociological positions, and the words functionalism and positivism, which were used (how accurately is open to argument) to identify the dominant tendencies in 1940s/1950s sociology, became abuse terms. The criticism of these dominant tendencies took many forms. They were criticized for ideological and social conformity, for example. Much of the criticism took a philosophical form, and many of the arguments in the 1960s were about the epistemological status of the different points of view. Did they, that is, fit with defensible conceptions of what knowledge could be? Did they, specifically, rest on adequate conceptions of how knowledge of social phenomena could be acquired?

Ethnomethodology came to the attention of the sociological public in the 1960s, and it seemed to provide the most drastic critique of established sociological views. It seemed to be undermining the epistemological conceptions underlying positivist sociology and replacing them with a completely different set. At a time when people were competing as to who held the most radical positions, ethnomethodology seemed to go further than anyone else in rejecting all the assumptions that had been made about what sociology could and should be. It appeared to be so radical in its willingness to abandon the idea of sociology as a rigorous and objective science, and in its rejection of the methods and theories then available that it seemed, even then, to many people to have gone too far. However, if ethnomethodology did seem too extreme for many, nonetheless it caught their attention for it seemed to have put its finger on some serious problems at the very foundation of sociological thought, to have shown perhaps that there are limits to the extent that sociology can be objective, scientific in character.

First impressions of ethnomethodology were formed out of very little information. The first effects of it were often felt through rumour, for very few of its writing were accessibly published and the great bulk of ethnomethodologists were young graduate students or beginning teachers located in the various campuses of the University of California. Such writings about ethnomethodology as there were tended to be circulated as mimeographs amongst those already in the know, giving the impression of being a closed clique with cultish attitudes to these manuscripts, an impression which was to be and perhaps still is held against it. As more and more information about it leaked out, the impression that it presented a serious challenge to sociology that needed to be answered dissipated. Some, it is true, throught that it showed itself to be a challenge not just to sociology, but to the whole intellectual and social structure of the Western world, but many more came to see it as at least eccentric, even very silly, and the fact of the concentration of its membership in California became a basis for deriding it: there were many modish and foolish things going on in and coming out of California in the 1960s and this was one of them. The impression grew that it was just a kind of game-playing. Harold Garfinkel would have his students do 'experiments', what were in reality demonstrations for classroom purposes of what is involved in sociological ideas. These were breach experiments, they required students to do things which went against conventional expectations in various small, but often disturbing ways. Thus, students were called upon to act like lodgers in their own homes, to bargain over the price of goods in stores, to violate the rules of games like chess and tic-tak-toe, to surprise people by revealing themselves to have just tape-recorded the conversation they were having and so on. These 'experiments' were useful illustrative devices, no more, and they were certainly not meant to be taken, as they so often were, as showing what ethomethodology was all about. These experiments became the focus of a stigmatizing stereotype: ethnomethodology was an excuse to do silly things, play provocative games.

As more and more of the writing became available, and as ethnomethodologists took the opportunity to travel that their increasing notoriety provided them with, so the expectations about ethnomethodology tended to be increasingly disappointing for many people. Ethnomethodologists often seemed more like empiricists than people of philosophical and theoretical sophistication. They did not want to talk about foundational issues at all, usually, but insisted that people should pay attention to the data, to various odd fragments of material that they had. When those who had undertaken the development of conversational analysis came into contact with the wider sociological community, this impression was confirmed: here were people who looked with unvelievably close attention at bits of transcriptions of tape recordings of ordinary conversation and whose discussion never seemed to rise more than the odd inch above the level of those materials. If there was disappointment that something which had promised something profound turned out, after all, not to deliver, there was probably also a great sigh of relief: something which might have called upon us to completely turn around our conception of sociology need not be taken all that seriously. If the philosophical orientations of ethnomethodology appeared to call for an intellectual revolution in sociology, then its applications to sociological studies produced trivial and uninteresting findings: if conversational analysis was the consequence of ethnomethodology, then there was nothing there that reoriented sociology in a promising and interesting direction.

Interest evaporated. A hard core of ethnomethodologists and conversational analysts have gone their own way, but they are relatively few in number, and their work now attracts little, if any, attention from other sociologists. They are often pursuing just the kinds of sociology that ethnomethodology would have appeared to rule out—Marxism and structuralism being two main tendencies. They are aware that ethnomethodology would offer certain criticisms of this, but feel secure that such criticisms can be set aside. Though ethnomethodology offers radical objections, they lack real force.

Ethnomethodology is not a product of 1960s California at all, nor is it an invitation to make a nonsense out of sociology or an incitement to silly behaviour at cocktail parties. Our aim in this little book is to show that it is a reasoned and serious approach to the issues of sociology, and that the problems that it raised have not, in most sociological circles, been understood, let alone answered. More importantly, they have not been overcome. Sociologists may feel that ethnomethodology has been answered, that arguments have been given which defend other conceptions of sociology against it, or which invalidate its main claims, but it cannot be argued that sociology has overcome the problems with which ethnomethodology was concerned. Those problems persist, are just as chronic now as they were in the 1960s when controversy was at its height. As we shall point out, ethnomethodology was particularly intrigued by the methodological difficulties of sociology, by the way in which its researches repeatedly fall short of their own targets, and the situation is, as far as that is concerned, virtually unchanged. We will do our best to dispel the impression that ethnomethodology's importance is no more than that of a passing fad.

What needs to be emphasized is the extent to which ethnomethodology is Harold Garfinkel's creature, and that it is best understood as the product of his amazingly patient and single-minded pursuit of a sociological possibility. He not only identified the possibility, but also saw just how it could be systematically explored, and just how it could be applied. He has over the years been surrounded by collaborators and students, and his work has inspired others to give their own slant to the idea or implications of ethnomethodology, but hard core ethnomethodological thinking must be defined relative to Garfinkel's persistent commitment to pushing the line of thought as far as it will go. The only other figure of comparable creativity in this area is the late Harvey Sacks, who showed a single-mindedness and inventiveness comparable to Garfinkel's own but who applied that almost entirely to one line of empirical investigation, into the organization of ordinary conversation. Many others have done work of high quality and originality, but its motivation and achievements have been defined in terms of the framework of ethnomethodology created by Garfinkel, and of conversational analysis as developed by Sacks.

Ethnomethodology's boom period was certainly the 1960s and the location of that boom was unquestionably the California campuses, Garfinkel having gone to the Los Angeles campus in 1954. There a whole crop of graduate students were attracted to Garfinkel's work, some through the mediating influence of Aaron Cicourel, whose own book *Method and Measurement in Sociology* (1964) had been the first to give ethnomethodology real impact outside its own circles and to create the impression that a devastating critique of received sociological conceptions was possible. Garfinkel had associates, such as Edward Rose and Egon Bittner, whose occupational seniority was something comparable to his own, but most of those attracted to it were, like (to name a few) David Sudnow, Roy Turner,

Harvey Sacks, Don Zimmerman, Lawrence Wieder, Melvin Pollner, Howard Schwartz, both young and junior. Unquestionably the expansion of sociology, and particularly its growth on the prosperous California scene, was conductive to the accumulation of a following around ethnomethodology there, the network of relations amongst the campuses, staff and graduate students ensuring that Garfinkel's work would be heard about, and that graduate students often attempting empirical, ethnographic type work of their own, but loath to accept functionalist and positivist schemes, would be willing to look at something which offered an alternative to them. Likewise, the lectures which Harvey Sacks was giving from around 1964 on at the Irvine campus, attracted notice and were circulated in transcript.

Ethnomethodology did not, though, originate in California, nor do its concerns have anything specific to do with its subsequent location there. It originated from Garfinkel's time as a graduate student himself at Harvard in the 1940s, as a result of an encounter between American sociology and European social theory and philosophy, particularly the kind called phenomenology. The dominant theorist in American sociology at that time was Talcott Parsons, whose own preoccupations had developed out of his studies in Europe and his encounter with the social theory of Max Weber, Emile Durkheim and others. Parsons had sought to identify a convergence in fundamental views amongst many European theorists, to specify those views and to make his own theory a direct development of them. However, Parsons's own assumptions about philosophy and theory were of a Kantian kind, but there was available an alternative philosophical background to be had from the European continent, which had already been applied to an examination of the assumptions of social theory. Alfred Schutz and Aron Gurwitsch, two European scholars in exile in the USA had sought to expose the problems in the philosophical foundations of sociology and psychology respectively: Schutz had begun with a re-examination of the bases of Max Weber's thought and, in America, had begun to consider, in the same way, the work of G. H. Mead and Parsons himself. Both Schutz and Gurwitsch had drawn their inspiration from the phenomenology of Edmund Husserl, a point of view developed and evolving through the first decades of the twentieth century. Whatever one might think of Parsons sociological theories themselves, one can admire the determination with which Parsons sought to think his way systematically through a problem and its implications over a long period, forty years and more. Garfinkel himself set out to think, no less thoroughly or systematically, through similar basic problems about the foundations of sociological thought, and began to do this by going over the work of Parsons, but starting out from the very different set of philosophical assumptions that phenomenology provided as compared to those which Parsons had employed. In a sense, it was entirely contigent that Parsons provided the materials for Garfinkel's re-thinking of sociological suppositions: other sociological works would have done as well, though Parsons's own determination to push things through as thoroughly and as far as he could perhaps made him especially useful as a sounding board. Though Garfinkel was critical of Parsons, it was always from a position of immense respect, and he would certainly never have aligned himself with the contemptuous dismissals that were often given of Parsonian theory. From Garfinkel's point of view Parsons squares up, as well as anybody and better than most, to basic problems.

Let us just add, however, that Garfinkel's was not an encounter at the level of theory alone. He was aware of the empirical aspect of American sociology and of the numerous attempts to develop research techniques, to devise methods for describing, classifying, recording and quantifying sociological data, and he was therefore always attuned, in a way Parsons was not, to the necessity not just to think theoretically, but also to be aware of the problem of relating theory to research, of the need to think about the relationship between the theoretical system and the techniques of data collection, organization and analysis.

PHENOMENOLOGY AND ETHNOMETHODOLOGY

Though Garfinkel was himself heavily and directly influenced by phenomenology, it is not absolutely essential that, in order to understand and practice ethnomethodology, one have a comparable involvement with or attachment to it. Nonetheless, something may usefully said about the background phenomenology provides because an understanding of this will give a much clearer idea about some of the moves ethnomethodology makes and, what is even more important, about some of the basic attitudes it takes.

Phenomenology was as much Husserl's creature as ethnomethodology Garfinkel's. Husserl was disappointed by tendencies in philosophy as he saw them at the end of the nineteenth century. There had been a degeneration of philosophy, reducing it from the distinctive, autonomous and deep inquiry that it had been in the hands of the great philosophers into something that was little more than a handmaiden to the natural sciences. The views of the kind called positivist were a particular affront: they vaunted the findings of science as though these provided the only possible kind of knowledge, and gave philosophy the job of, at best, clearing the way to speed the progress of scientific knowledge. Though not denigrating the natural sciences, Husserl insisted that the kind of empirical, contingent knowledge that they provided was not the understanding of the essentials of things that philosophy had sought, nor did science achieve the kind of certainty upon whose possibility the greater philosophers had pondered. The tasks of philosophy were certainly not to be defined by the natural sciences. Indeed, the boot was on the other foot: it was philosophy's job to look into the foundational presuppositions of the sciences, since the sciences themselves were not aware of and could not examine them.

His own philosophy was meant to take up the task pursued by René Descartes, the search for certainty, a quest for those truths which would be self-evident and which could not be doubted. Of course, there are many things that we take for truths in our ordinary lives or because we are attached to given philosophical or scientific theories, but for Husserl, as for Descartes, these may not be genuine truths and may be open to doubt. One cannot, therefore, begin by accepting anything as already given: one has to *establish* where the certainties lie and one must therefore withdraw allegiance from all suppositions that one can abandon. The aim is to bring presuppositions to consciousness and to see which, if any of them, one is compelled to accept. Therefore phenomenology involves an unremitting effort to make a completely new beginning. The assumptions and suppositions of phenomenology are not to be defined by other philosophies and theories, and philosophy cannot therefore accept as given the terms which they offer. It must seek to begin its inquiries in a location outside the frameworks provided by established theories. One such location is in the world of our pre-theoretical experinece, with the world as we ordinarily experience it *before* we start to theorize about it. The unprejudiced examation of the world as it is found in our ordinary experience is something to which phenomenology devotes itself, under the slogan 'to the things themselves' in order that it may see more clearly what the relationship between the world and our theories about it actually is. Even this capsule account of the motivation of phenomenology shows why (a) ethnomethodology is likely to feel itself distanced from the main tendencies in sociology's thinking and (b) why those who are attached to those tendencies should have difficulty in comprehending what ethnomethodology is about.

Husserl's programme meant that he could not sign up with the successful tradition of scientific inquiry which, called 'Galilean science' after its great innovator, was increasingly regarded as the standard of knowledge. He could not accept that tradition any more than he could accept any other as given-without-examination, by the very nature of his own approach: whatever presumptions might be provided by that science could not be unthinkingly taken over. The object of his inquiry was, as much as anything, to see what the foundations of such a science were, and an inquiry into those required distance from and neutrality toward them, not acceptance of or dependence on them. The positivist philosophy which sought to recommend, defend and advance the cause of Galilean science could not be accepted either, for it would require that philosophy be, in a way Husserl would not accept, defined by the problems of the natural sciences. Consequently, ethnomethodology, following after the phenomenological example, will also find itself apart from some main assumptions of sociology, especially those which envisage that sociology must follow in the path of Galilean science and which seek to imbue the discipline with a positivist spirit.

The distancing from the assumptions of Galilean science is, we have said, nothing personal: it is part and parcel of the policy of declining *all* pregiven theories insofar as this can be done. However, the refusal to sign up with the positivist position is often taken as involving a rejection of the findings of Galilean science, a refusal to recognize that they provide knowledge. Thus phenomenology, and ethnomethodology after it, are likely to be looked upon as attempting to deny what are, from the point of view of Galilean science/positivist philosophy, the unarguable findings and results issuing from the laboratories. However, withholding assent is not the same as arguing against, and the fact is that the phenomenological exercise is done in the name of clarification, in pursuit of (among other things) a clearer conception of how theories relate to the world as we experience it. The intent is certainly not to offer alternative theories or results to those provided by Galilean science, but to examine the presuppositions of that tradition of inquiry.

Ethnomethodology has, then, something of an uncompromising character. One of the ways in which it puzzles is in its disposition to 'rock the boat', seemingly wanting to question everything and refusing to accept what seem quite reasonable things to everyone else. This is not some quirk of personality, but a product of the methodological influence of phenomenology. That something is reasonable and plausible and seemingly correct does not make it acceptable to phenomenology, which wants to put questions about what we *must* accept, rather than what we might accept. Thus, it is perfectly possible to argue a reasonable case about how we can approach sociology, such as (say, for the sake of argument) from a functionalist point of view, but ethnomethodologhy will want to ask whether we have to approach it from this point of view: are the assumptions of functionalist inquiry *definitive* of the sociological point of view? Or are there alternatives to them? Thus, Parsons's own sociological approach may be a perfectly reasonable and viable one, but the fact that it defines the possibilities of inquiry in one way leaves open the possibility that they can be defined entirely differently. Unless we have explored the range of possible basic assumptions that can be made about the sociological project, we are not clear about what we are doing in choosing any one. Unless we have worked through the implications of the choices available to us, then again in an important sense we do not know what we are doing in making choices.

Ethnomethodology does not set out to accomplish the same tasks as previous sociological theories have done. Examining the fundamental assumptions of sociology is as much a matter of inspecting the roster of tasks as it is of appraising ways of doing them. Objectives, as well as methods, are open to examination. Ethnomethodology does not therefore take on board a defined set of objectives, for the location of objectives will be a product of its inquiries, not the condition of it. Hence it is absurd to look in the way many sociologists do at ethnomethodology as if it were trying to do the same things they do, to give explanations in the ways that they do. Seen in such an absurd fashion, ethnomethodology will itself look absurd. Far from seeing how well ethnomethodology is doing at the traditional tasks of sociology one should recognize how different are the tasks it has set itself from which sociology conventionally pursues. It is, in many respects, dealing with tasks of the first instance. In the first instance for example, it wants to examine the process of sociological theorizing. It is not much interested in the content of theories nor in providing a theory of its own, but is interested much more in the fact that the social world is available to theoretical formulation: how can the world be conceived in terms of a theory, how can a theory engender findings, results, discoveries? How is sociological theorizing done? Alfred Schutz had begun such inquiries: he asked how there was an orderly, intelligible social reality there to theorize about, and how sociological theorizing could begin in its midst. He began, therefore, with the effort to show how the unstructured flow of pure experience could come to be comprehended in terms of schemes of typifications, i.e. how anyone could come to experience, and formulate in language, the character of the world of daily life as a scene of typical occurrences and situations, produced for typical reasons by typical kinds of people. The phenomena of sociology, he argued, were *already and intrinsically* typified, and sociology itself must therefore be counted a 'second order discipline', building further typifications on and in addition to those already available in society itself. Thus, for Garfinkel it is *practical sociological reasoning* which is one of the central topics of his investigation, and the way in which professional sociologist's reasoning is subsumed under that.

Garfinkel cannot, any more than phenomenology can, begin within the framework of anyone else's theory, cannot address phenomena as they are defined through someone else's scheme of thought: he, too, seeks to identify a place in which to begin inquiries which is outside of the theoretical and methodological givens of the main sociological traditions. He begins, therefore, with the world of our commonplace experience, the social world of daily life. This leads many sociologists to accuse ethnomethodology of subjectivism, of being concerned with how things appear to us rather than with how they really are in themselves. Indeed, the name phenomenology itself echoes Kant's distinction between noumena, or things as they are in themselves, and phenomena, or things as they appear to us: phenomenology is the study of things as they appear to us, of our consciousness of the world. In order to further inquiry into this, phenomenology adopts a technique of 'bracketing' i.e. of suspending judgement on the veracity of our experiences in order that we may concentrate on identifying the character and structure of the world *as experienced*. Ethnomethodology, analogously gives its attention to the study of the social world as encountered in everyday experience, the world as it appears to our common sense and, likewise, attempts to bracket further questions about whether the social world really is as it appears.

At various points we will show that ethnomethodology is repeatedly misunderstood as taking one side of various dilemmas when if fact it rejects these dilemmas. Thus, it is criticized for being preoccupied with subjective phenomena, as indeed it seems to be insofar as it elects to examine the world of our everyday experience: after all social reality might not be as it appears to us, our common understandings may be mistaken. However, to see this as recommending a concern with experience at the expense of the-world-as-it-really-is-independent-of-our-experience is to preserve the very dualism of our experience and the world that phenomenology is trying to get around. The aim is not to displace objectivity with subjective experience but to discover how objectivity can originate in experience. Concentration on our consciousness of the world does not involve a concentration on consciousness instead of the world, but rather a recognition of the fundamental feature of consciousness, that it is intentional (or directed outward): consciousness is directed, so to speak, at the world, it is characteristically consciousness-of-something, consciousness of something other than itself. It is only by beginning with the world as we are conscious of it that we can understand how it is possible for us to get from the world-as-it-appears to the-world-as-it-really-is-in-itself. These phenomenological impulses lead ethnomethodology to look at precisely how the world of daily life is experienced to see just how it is possible for there to be that phenomenon which is basic to the classic, Durkheimian, conception of sociology, viz. the social world *experienced* as an objective environment because it is, of course, a most basically notable feature of our common sense experience that it encounters the social world as an *objective given*.

We have tried, with this thumbnail sketch of phenomenology to suggest that ethnomethology's apparent awkwardness is other than just perversity and to intimate why some of the conflicts and misunderstandings that follow on from it have done so. However, before we conclude this chapter two things need to be done. First, we need to point out that Garfinkel's pursuit of the phenomenological programme and his espousal of the cause of Alfred Schutz do not mark him out as the sole guardian of phenomenological tradition nor even necessarily as its legitimate inheritor. Schutz himself and others, like Maurice Natanson, had seen that phenomenology had implications for the social sciences and had tried to draw attention to these, though these efforts were for a long time peripheral to and unnoticed by sociology.

It was in the 1960s that Schutz began to receive attention, and the rapid rediscovery of his writings was probably due more to the publication of Peter Berger and Thomas Luckmann's *The Social Construction of Reality* (1966) than to the notoriety of ethnomethodology. Berger and Luckmann sought to found a reconsideration of the sociology of knowledge in Schutz's pre-sociological reflections, using those as a platform for a reconciliation, as complementary moments of a dialectrical process, of society as subjective and society as objective reality, this being, in fact, a matter of showing complementarity in the views of such seemingly opposed theorists as Karl Marx and G. H. Mead. We do not take a greater interest in Garfinkel than in Berger and Luckmann because he is necessarily more of a true or approved inheritor of Schutz's tradition but because he was the one who saw the potential for a much more radical rethinking of sociological ideas in the work of Schutz. Thus, Berger and Luckmann work within the framework of recieved theories, those of Marx, Mead, Durkheim and Weber for example, and within the problems as defined by these, seeking reconciliation of differences without examining the context in which those oppositions arise. Garfinkel, by contrast, sees the phenomenological option as opening up the possibility of stepping *completely* outside the framework of given sociological theory. Further, Berger and Luckmann's efforts remained at the level of a philosophical/theoretical re-interpretation and did not involve as Garfinkel's did, an attempt to push the rethinking right through, so that it would transform the conception of an empirical sociological investigation just as much as the idea of what were necessary theoretical presuppositions.

The second and concluding point that we want to make is that acceptance of phenomeology is not a necessary presentation of sympathy for ethnomethodology, and some ethnomethodologists are pretty cool about phenomenology. Some find no need for philosophical inspiration, others find that insofar as that is what is wanted they can get as much and better from the so-called ordinary language philosophers such as Ludwig Wittgenstein, Gilbert Ryle and J. L. Austin. The latter was sometimes willing to describe what he did as a kind of linguistic phenomenology but the other two were sharply critical of phenomenology. However, one can find in the writings of Wittgenstein, Ryle and Austin much the same kind of motivation as Garfinkel found in Husserl to radically reconsider received doctrines, the same uncompromising insistence on being clear about just what one *has* to accept, the same desire to look again, afresh and independently of preconceived theories at the phenomena of commonplace experience, and the same willingness to engage in unconstructive exercises that are perhaps never expected to construct theories or result in findings.

2

Some Preliminary Considerations

In the first chapter, we briefly indicated that some critics have quite a dislike of ethnomethodology and its programme of studies. Part of the task which we have set outselves in this chapter is to indicate how mistaken many of the initial reactions to ethnomethodology are and how far they misunderstand the nature of the work being carried out. In particular, we will try to show that the demonstrations and studies which many find baffling, if not downright distasteful, were designed by Garfinkel to bring home to his students what he feels to be a crucial weakness in the foundations of contemporary and classical sociology. The conclusion that sociology was flawed in this way was not lightly arrived at. Nor is the significance which Garfinkel gives to it easily appreciated. It was the culmination of an arduous, painstaking and lengthy examination of what for him was the most systematic, thorough, integrated and theoretically powerful sociological schemes available, namely that of Talcott Parsons. The significance he gives the conclusion he draws is simply that if one accepts the characterization of the problem as Garfinkel gives it, then it will be no longer possible to carry on with the sociological investigations and theorizing in the same ways. To do so, to close ones eyes and ignore the problem, would be an act of bad faith. We would have sacrificed the scholarly standards of the discipline in favour of an easy life.

Before we move on to the detail of Garfinkel's arguments and the conclusions which he draws, it might be as well to give one or two preliminary observations about the manner of our presentation. We will set out the case that ethnomethodology seeks to make as if it were a linear argument. To achieve this, we will have to jiggle with history a little. We will set up the early discussions as if they had a relentless, stepwise, progressive character with decision following decision cumulatively. We very well know that, historically, the developments were more accidental than that. We have already discussed something of the historical and intellectual milieux in which Garfinkel and others were working in the review we gave in Chapter 1. However, we have taken our task to be the presentation of ethnomethodology's case in what we take to be as cogent a manner as possible. This is, then, our view. It is how we think the various strands and arguments can be most readily collected together and given a common motivation.

The second thing to say right at the start is that we are very well aware that it is possible to disagree with Garfinkel and his conclusion that sociology as conventionally pursued must be put to one side. Many, including those like Parsons for whom Garfinkel has nothing but the most profound respect, disagree with him. They are not convinced by his arguments, nor do they accept that his worries are as important as he thinks. They would put things differently and distribute emphases in ways that are different to his. Neither we, nor Garfinkel, would want to deny their right to make the choices which they do. All that is being said, and here we would want to draw attention to the often unnoticed reasonableness of ethnomethodology, is that if certain choices are made then certain consequences follow. The question is not whether one can make those choices but whether one has to do so. Garfinkel, imbibing something of the spirit of phenomenologys concern with investigating foundations, asks that question. He will hold nothing sacred. There is nothing which cannot be raised for scrutiny. The result of this scrutiny is a re-drawing of the baselines of the discipline, its premisses, and then the systematic following through of their implications. In its own view, and, agreed, not everyone shares it, ethnomethodology has a 'foundational' relationship with more conventional sociology, i.e. it inquires into what they would regard as their foundations. These differences then work their way through such important aspects as the role of theory, the nature of data, the place of studies, and much, much more.

Let us begin with a point of agreement. Nearly everyone, no matter what their theoretical interests, will accept that whatever other aspirations sociology might have, it is empirical in intent. It makes studies of the real social world which exists out there, independent of each of us. This much everyone shares with Durkheim. It makes these studies by investigating what it defines as sociological phenomena. There are, of course, many different views of what this term is supposed to mean. At the broadest level, and hence the proposal is not all that informative, one might say that sociology's topic is the organization of social activities or patterns of social life. There are many ways in which this general topic might be taken up. You might choose, for example, to be most interested in finding out about some delineated area of social life such as the distribution of power in democratic societies or changes in fertility over the past 50 years. Such a researcher's interests might be contrasted with those of a theorist who would primarily be concerned with conceptualizing the overall pattern of activities in terms of sets of related concepts and processes. Both of these two are quite distinct from an interest in the problem of operationalizing, with itemizing and specifying the steps which have to be taken in order to carry out studies of some phenomenon. None of these choices is, of course, more important, worthy or foundational for sociology than any of the others. However, once the choice has been made, important consequences follow. If, for instance, it was the issue of operationalizing which you wished to pursue, what would that imply? Well, first of all it might mean that you would not be all that committed to any one theory for its own sake. You would not feel it necessary to stay with the theory, elaborate it, see how it works out under all circumstances. Your interest would be in cashing theories in, so-to-speak, in seeing what actual empirical value they might have. Theories, in your view, would simply be means to the end of making studies. Neither would you be committed, as a researcher might be, to a particular range of topics or segment of the social world or to a particular investigative technique. For you, it is a matter of matching theories, research practices and domains of inquiry. Most particularly what will concern you is how to make certain that a set of research practices actually does get to grips with the phenomenon it is designed for, the phenomenon articulated in the theory. If we might paraphrase a slogan of the late Mao Tse-tung, for you it would be 'Operationalism to the fore!' rather than theory or research.

Let us add a third, related attitude to those we have just set out. Let us suppose that what bothers you most about the procedures usually adopted when theories are operationalized in conventional research practices is the difficulty of preserving in sociological studies the feel or ambience that some activities might have for the ordinary persons involved in them. The things that characterize ordinary activities for those engaged in them seem to disappear whenever sociological theories and methods are brought into play. Whenever sociologists talk about family life, work, leisure and the rest, they seem to change the subject and discuss things that we as ordinary people would not recognize. In fact, in order to decipher what is being discussed, even sociologists have to refer back to their ordinary knowledge and experience of social life.

Here is a very brief and crude example of what we mean. We have twisted it a little so that it makes the point. Recently, some sociologists have become very much concerned with the nature of the professional–client relationship. They have done so because of the spread of professionaliza- tion into many new areas of life. Some have seen the professional–client relationship as typified by imbalances of power. In many subtle ways, the professional is able to exert domination over the client. Others prefer to view the relationships as ceremonial. Both parties exchange presentations of one sort or another. Knowledge and expertise are exchanged for deference, for example. Now it is perfectly possible to see the relationship between a doctor and his patient in these terms. Indeed many interesting sociological insights may be yielded. But, what gets pushed into the background, perhaps even lost altogether, is the obvious and mundane fact that what is going on is a medical encounter of some sort. If we treat the medical encounter as an instance of professional domination or ceremonial exchange, then what makes it medical and not, say, legal, or economic, will have been demoted or lost.

We can see the same sort of process at work if we approach things from the other end, namely the practicalities of research. Suppose that for perfectly good research reasons, you are committed to collecting data of a particular kind. Just to be even-handed, let us suppose that your are convinced that video-taping was the best way to preserve data for analysis. You tape record a number of consultations. You transcribe the exchanges and count the number of times the doctor elicits information by smiles and nods, the number of times the patient initiates new topics, the coordination of eye contact and head movements. Again the same question can be asked. Fascinating as the detailed observations may be, where has the medicine gone? What makes this two-party exchange different from any other? What makes it specifically this exchange? The point is, of course, if one was interested in the problems of operationalizing studies, one would become sensitive to this disappearance and one might ask if it has to happen. You might ask what it is that enables any one of us when confronted by sociological theories and research, to make sense of what is being said by recourse to our own experience.

It is our view that Garfinkel is probably best understood if he is approached by being sensitive to the problem of operationalizing studies. This does not mean that he has no interest in theory or research. But, his views can be seen to have a rationale if they are taken as attempts to work out how to do sociological studies which do not lead to the disappearance of the phenomenon. The proposals he makes and the reasons for them are nowhere near as straightforward as the problem seems to be. To appreciate them, we will first have a look at what Garfinkel takes the character of theorizing to be as well as the nature of research. Only then can we move on to see how he applies these views in his own studies.

The interest in operationalizing theories is not quite so arbitrary as we have perhaps made it sound. If you are interested in the relationship between a theory and the world, then it would normally be assumed that you are interested in the question of whether the theory corresponds to the world, whether what the theory says about the world is true of it. If the correspondence between a theory and the things it is about is to be assessed, however, this will have to be done through research, through the making of investigations which will establish how things are, and if they are indeed as the theory says. Methods of research are not neutral between theories, for a theory, since it has ideas about how the world is, must also have ideas about what it will take to establish facts about it. The question about the operationalization of a theory is, then, a question about what it takes to make the world investigable *in terms of the theory*. The correspondence between what a theory says and how things are is one connection between theory and world, but checking on that requires another, more primordial link which enables us to say what kind of observable occurrences in the world would count as fulfilling or disqualifying the claims of the theory and how these might be identified and specified. This primordial connection is made through the operationalizing of the theory, and given ethnomethodology's commitment to searching out the most basic connections, then these rather than the substantive claims of a theory provide an appropriate place to start.

A few sentences ago, we introduced the notion of bad faith and suggested that to carry on with established procedures even though one recognized they were inadequate by their own standards would be an example of bad faith because it would be a rejection of scholarly standards. For Garfinkel it is the absence of bad faith which characterizes the very best sociological theories we have. Bad faith will not pursue a theory to uncomfortable conclusions, will not accept results which counter the preferable options, will not follow through a line of argument come what may. Bad faith wants theorizing to be easy and straightforward. But good theories are not easy to find, nor is theorizing lightly to be entered into. Laying out a set of theoretical tenets and following them through ought to be no haphazard affair. It requires that very precise steps be taken and very strict rules observed. But even then we are not out of the wood. Once we have taken the steps and satisfied the rules, there is still the problem of operationalizing the theory so that the phenomena within its purview do not disappear as soon as we engage in research.

From the point of view of operationalization, the most important thing a theory can have is clarity. All of the components and their relationships should be easily visible. The whole structure of reasoning embedded in the theory ought to be on view. Anyone should, at least in principle, be able to work out all of the moves and all of the steps for themselves. In Garfinkel's case, the concern with clarity is expressed as a request that theories be set out so that they are comprehensible on their own terms to anyone who comes to them. We will introduce this idea now in a way that will probably seem a bit odd. However, once we have worked our way through the argument, it will seem a lot easier to grasp. For Garfinkel, it ought to be possible to treat sociological theories as sets of instructions for the production of social life. As with all good sets of instructions, the directions contained in these instructions should be precise and easily followed. In terms of theory, the latter point means that whenever a decision is made within a theory or on behalf of a theory, it ought to be possible to say why that particular theoretical choice was made and what its consequences are. There is one thing to notice here which is massive in its implications. In treating theories as sets of instructions, Garfinkel does not define theories as explanations nor evaluate them in terms of the explanatory power. The predisposition to presume theories to be explanations is just one of the central premises he wishes to question. Following phenomenology, Garfinkel asks what a descriptive discipline would consist in. Conventionally, sociology sees itself as explanatory in character. The divergence mirrors that between phenomenology and most other of philosophy which we mentioned in Chapter 1. As we will see in our concluding chapter, the failure to see this distinctive definition of theory has led many critics to make the quite misplaced allegation that ethnomethodology fails to account for or explain social life. It cannot fail to do that which it does not attempt.

What is it that bad faith is indicative of? In very broad terms, we could say it is a disregard for the rules of theorizing and the use of theory within the discipline. It is very difficult to define these rules. Certainly they are not regulations and are more like a set of commitments which sociologists and other social scientists seem to respect and perhaps even advocate. The philosopher Felix Kaufmann codified these rules as he saw them in a book, *The Methodology of the Social Sciences,* which was very influential on Garfinkel. We might summarize their outline in a set of three maxims.

(1) When employing a theory, use only those terms defined in the theory.
(2) Use only coherent, consistent and rigorous theories.
(3) Use only theories which yield studies of real phenomena.

The most obvious thing to say about these maxims is that they are not at odds with a conception of theory and method which we might call empiricist in orientation. The canons of logicality, consistency, realism and so on could well be those derived from Galilean science.

Despite what is often said, arriving at one sociological theory which satisfies all of these maxims would be no easy matter. In Garfinkel's view, we would be lucky if many of our current theories satisfied one or at most two. Why is this? Why is it that the theories we have seem to fail to meet the standards which they set themselves? As we shall see, it is Garfinkel's opinion that the failure results from a mismatch of aspirations and premises. His conclusion is that one or other must be sacrificed. Ethnomethodology is the working through of an alternative set of premises to achieve the aspirations stated. We will now see how he arrives at that conclusion. In the next chapter, we will see what his alternative sets of premises are composed of.

(1) Use only terms defined within a theory

This maxim is a generally accepted one. What Garfinkel does is to view it from what we called the phenomenological point of view. From that point of view, what the maxim expresses is what Husserl calls the theoretical attitude. The phenomena which are the subject of theorizing are viewed from the point of view of the theory and *only* the point of view of the theory. All other considerations are deemed to be irrelevant or are bracketed off. For Husserl, the theoretical attitude was essential to science and could be seen in all scientific theories. Which terms were to be included within the thory was for the theorist to decide. In this sense, the theorist constructs a world *by fiat*. However, once the terms have been decided upon and the methods for dealing with them laid out, the theorist is bound by his stipulations. He cannot ignore them, subvert them or seek to redefine them without working out what such redefinition means all the way through. In this sense, therefore, it is possible to say that the theorist knows nothing other than what is specified in the theory. Any knowledge which he may have as an ordinary member of the society in which he lives should be put on one side.

The distinctiveness of the theoretical attitude can be brought out quite easily. In many sociological accounts of legal processes, the actors which populate the legal system, lawyers, judges, policemen, defendants and so on are not real people, but social types. Thus one can talk of the role of the lawyer without any reference to the personal characteristics of individual lawyers. One does not need to know the firm they are associated with, their specialism, date of birth, or even gender. For a lot of sociological purposes, these characteristics are irrelevant. From the point of view of the theory, the persons who occupy the role of lawyer are more or less interchangeable. It does not matter exactly who the particular lawyer might be. From the point of view of someone dealing with a real-life legal problem, however, lawyers are anything butinterchangeable social types. Such a person will be interested in the particularities of individual lawyers (are they good? are they expensive? are they sympathetic? what is their speciality? etc.) and what exactly is known about individuals. The treatment they get from the legal system might very well depend upon the particular lawyer they use.

It seems then that sociology adopts an attitude towards social life which views it as providing a field of resources, for example types of actions and types of actors, which can be called into play in theories. As we mentioned just now, such theories could be said to be descriptions or accounts of social life. Because we are interested in theories as descriptions and not as explanations, we cannot talk in terms of *the* theory of this or that aspect of social life. No theory has pride of place. At the same time, this does not mean that we can never find a theory to be useless, limited or even false. It simply means that the criterion for the acceptablility of a theory is its descriptive adequacy. If to secure such adequacy, we have to make adjustments, extensions and redefinitions by invoking terms not defined in the theory itself then it is the theory which will have to be sacrificed. We cannot save a theory simply because we want it to work, or because we wish it could accommodate recalcitrant data. It must stand or fall on its own terms.

An example from around the house might make this a bit clearer. Anyone who has central heating knows that occasionally, particularly when the system has been switched off for a long time, radiators can get air-locked. This is the effect of the causal properties of the water in the central heating system. It expands when hot and contracts when cool; it seeks its own level; air is only weakly dissolvable in it, and so on. We do not attribute the coldness of our radiators when we turn the system on to the malign influence of the spirit world, witchcraft by our enemies, or an unaccountable hiccough in the laws of nature. From the point of view of very simple physical theory, there is no room for and no need to resort to explanations of that kind. This does not mean, of course, that physics is static. But, whatever changes we want to introduce to this kind of simple theory must be consonant with the stipulations it is committed to.

(2)   Use only logically consistent, coherent and rigorous theories

Just now we suggested that ad hoc adjustments to save a theory seemed to be ruled out by our first maxim. This is because that maxim is usually used in tandem with the second. This second maxim brings out the important feature that theories are not just collections of theses, propositions and the rest lumped together in a random fashion. Theories ought to be constructed following particular procedural rules. The two most important of these rules seem to be:

(i) theories should be composed of the simplest possible elements which are aggregated in defined ways;
(ii) propositions within a theory should all mesh together.

The combination of these two procedural rules is held to underpin the rigour of a theory.

For many, this is a distinctive use of the notion of rigour. Often, rigour is defined in terms of exact measurement. A rigorous theory or a rigorous explanation is one to which exact tests and measurements have been applied. However, this use of the term is but an instance of the more general interpretation. A rigorous theory is one in which, by means of defined procedures, propositions can be systematically reduced to their elements. These elements are independent of each other. When combined these atomic propositions yield molecular and then compound ones. Theories became more and more general. We will see in the next chapter that it was precisely this sort of generalizing strategy which Parsons sought to borrow from the natural sciences.

Leaving aside clarity and consistency for the moment, it is clear that rigour is one standard which could be used to evaluate theories. We have already mentioned that Husserl wished to argue that Galilean science did not have rigorous foundations because it had not secured its elementary propositions. The reality of the object of perception which was the basis of Galilean science could be further reduced by the application of the phenomenological method. Garfinkel says the same thing about sociological theories. It is here that much of the misapprehension of ethnomethodology has its origin. Making the reductions, or at least seeing if they can be made, invokes asking which of the premises in hand can be suspended and which must remain in place. To do that it is necessary to step outside the more usual frameworks applied within sociological thinking and take what Schutz in a remark in a letter to Parsons called one more radical step. Once the step was taken, the consequence would be to change the character of sociological investigation. However, we will leave the demonstration of what that step is and how it was achieved to the next chapter.

The second rule we cited above says that a theory should be seamless. It must be consistent and coherent, with implications of the premises worked out all the way through. The steps to be taken within the theory, for example from level to level of generality, must be those set out in the stipulations. If alternative possible outcomes are available, these must be accounted for within the theory. Clearly what is crucial here is, once more, the range of theory. Standardly in sociology these boundaries have been signposted as the individual and society; the one defined by 'macro' social structures, the other by 'micro' ones. The task for any theory is then presumed to be the unification of the micro with the macro, showing how the individual fits into and yet makes up society. But, as is well known, no theory which attempts to provide this unity is wholly satisfactory. Rather like when the curious child takes a clock apart to see how it works and then tries to put it together again, there are always bits and pieces left over which seem to have no obvious place to fit in. Having given itself the puzzle of unifying the individual and society, sociology is left without a workable solution. Part of Garfinkel's stepping outside of the given frameworks defining sociology is, as we shall see, his determination to break away from the dichotomizing of the individual and society. Instead of seeking to move from the level of the ordinary life of the individual up to the level of macro social structure, Garfinkel begins by asking whether social structures can be made visible *within* ordinary life.

(3) Operationality with real phenomena

The point of theories is to lay out the possibilities for studies. Theories are means to better and better studies of real worldly phenomena. To some this may seem a little odd. For them, the point of studies is to validate, verify or test theories. Here there can be seen another influence of Husserl. The empiricist demand that theories be verifiable was, for Husserl, a consequence of the errors made by Galilean science. The whole hypothesis–test––verification logic assumed a constancy of the phenomenon. It was precisely this which Husserl rejected. Phenomena are constituted by theories and attitudes; not the other way round. The difficulties that the presumption of a constancy of the phenomenon raise for sociological methods were well known within the discipline, but more often than not regarded as troublesome but minor irritants which in time would pass away as methods became more and more subtle and sophisticated. It is only with the publication of Aaron V. Cicourel's *Method and Measurement in Sociology* that the discipline was made aware how deep-rooted the problems might be. Unfortunately, this book was taken as a contribution to the debates over method rather than an attempt to point out the debate's futility. What debates over the principles of method ignored were the real practical problems of achieving a measurement system that was consistent, or setting up an experiment which did what one wanted it to, or of conducting a survey with teams of assistants. The problems here were not those of sound method in a principled sense but of practical organizational management. The consequence of practical organizational management was what we earlier called the disappearance of the phenomenon. The requirement of objective data, measurement systems, consistency across investigators etc., etc. all led to the replacement of the phenomenon by artefacts of method––data runs, variables, indicators and the like.

As we indicated at the begining of this chapter, in Garfinkel's view, the requirement of operationalization is the preservation of the phenomenon in actual investigations. Studies should allow the investigator to 'follow the animal' as he puts it. If instead, the animal keeps disappearing from sight and in order to make sense of the studies made one has to invoke what anyone knows about the character of the society we live in, then it is time to reflect on the realtionship between theory and investigation. In so doing, it is not expected that some solution to this mismatching will be found. Rather than taking the problem head on, Garfinkel expects to find some way around it. This will be achieved, or so he thinks, by the reconstitution of the premisses for theorizing and investigation since it is the stipulations which sociology has laid upon itself which have generated the problem.

We have made rather a strong claim in this chapter. Despite all attempts to remedy matters, sociology seems unable to satisfy the aspirations it sets for itself. Even the most rigorous, systematic and specified modern sociological theory, that of Talcott Parsons, fails its own tests. Any attempt to apply his theoretical categories leads to the disappearance of the phenomenon under study. In the next chapter we will examine Garfinkel's diagnosis of why this should be and his recommendations for what action should be taken.

3

Radicalizing Parsons: Garfinkel's Sociological Project

In both of the previous chapters, we have made strong play of the reasonable character of Garfinkels sociological programme. We have also stressed, though, that the relationship of this programme to more conventional sociology is not straightforward or easy to grasp. Indeed, for many coming to *Studies in Ethnomethodology* for the first time, the whole conception of sociology looks mysterious if not totally bizarre. The reason for this is, as we have said, the simple fact that Garfinkel wishes to raise for scrutiny the very foundations of sociology. We will now try to bring out the reasons why he wants to do this.

The rough order in which we will take things is as follows. First we will lay down the base line, the conception of sociology's analytic tasks as these were defined for Garfinkel by the discipline. As we have pointed out in the previous chapter, by and large this can be identified with the work of Talcott Parsons and the Parsonsian solution to the problem of order. As is well known, Parsons attempts to build a theory which will account for the stability of social structures through the reproduction of social order via the internal, systematic relationships holding between those structures. The system of social action reproduces itself. To this theory, Garfinkel brings his proceduralizing interest. To make studies which use Parsons theoretical framework and which deal directly with the detail life, it would be necessary to find ways of making social structures visible within the flux of day-to-day activities. Garfinkel tries to achieve this proceduralizing in a number of studies, demonstrations and 'experiments'. In each and every case, specification of the theory in terms of the detail required proves impossible. The findings arrived at are incompatible with the expectations set up by the theory. This, then, provides Garfinkel with this project. How could the Parsonsian framework be radicalized so that the incompatibility of findings and theory could be avoided? Here we will turn to the resource which Garfinkel himself used, namely the philosophy of Alfred Schutz. In drawing out the implications of Schutz's sociology, we will concentrate primarily on what Garfinkel was able to retain of the Parsonian framework and what was, perforce, given up. We will close by sketching out what can be thought of as Garfinkel's general orienting conceptions. In the following chapters, we will show how these conceptions were used to guide actual studies.

What was the central sociological problem as Parson saw it? He called it the Hobbesian problem of order, but what exactly does that mean? Putting things very simply, we can say that Parsons defines the sociologist's task as the provision of an account of the coordination of activities. He feels this coordination is brought about by the motivated compliance of the parties to the activities. In short, we are able to do the things we do in social life because we are predisposed to act together in suitably interrelated ways. Putting it more concretely, what the sociologist has to do is to provide a theoretical framework which will show how you, or any social actor, can do such things as buy goods in a shop you have never used before, find your way around towns you have never visited before, and make phone-calls to people you have never even heard of before (among other things of course). The theory has to make these things the ordinary, routine, generally no-problem affairs that they are for us. It is the orderly character of our ordinary lives which is sociology's problem. It is that which is the problem of order. Since Parsons is an incurable theorist, as he himself admits, he approaches the question in theoretical terms. He asks, What are the elements of a sociological theory which make social life as we ordinarily know it possible? Why and how do we manage to get along with one another? Since Parsons defines theorizing in the classical mode and wants to unify and integrate the established theories of Durkheim, Weber and others, he opts for what could be called a top-down approach. While it is the orderly character of our daily lives which is the object of explanantion, the focus and weight of the explanation will be found at other levels. For Parsons, what has to be shown is how the system of social action reproduces itself through what we all do in our lives.

What Parsons offers is a synthesis of classical theory. In his view each of the components of classical theory tells but part of the story. The whole needs to be wedded or welded together. We can see where the questions in which we have a direct interest are located if we look at the broad sweep of his views. The components to be fitted together in viable general sociological theory of social actions:

(1) a conception of social action as both interpretive and rational which derives from Weber;
(2) a conception of emergent patterns of action as structured wholes which is taken from Durkheim;
(3) an analytic viewpoint which defines structures of action as systems with the emergent patterns being codifiable into a social system.

The net result of these conceptions is a view which defines social order as an internal property of the system of social action. But this internal property can only be viewed and described from a vantage point outside the system. The procedures of scientific method appropriately adapted will make such observations possible.

It is with this last point that Garfinkel begins. How could studies be made which will allow the observation of actual social structures? That is to say, Garfinkel begins by presuming that Parsons's theory is designed to be empirical in orientation. How could the structures which Parsons describes and accounts for in the theory be made visible within the actual flow of daily life? Since these are the pehnomena which we are attempting to study, unless they can be made visible in the activities which constitute our data, we will have fallen into the trap of causing our phenomenon to disappear as soon as we set out to investigate it. The essential properties of the phenomenon, the real-worldly objective character of social structure, should be both identified and preserved in the studies.

We suggested in the previous chapter that one way in which Garfinkel tries to bring out the problem here is to treat theories as if they embodied sets of instructions for the production of social life. If we looked at Parsons in this way, what would this mean for his theory? To begin with, of course, we would have to identify the level at which the instructions were to apply. Although, it might be important to study society in general, or the system as a whole, or even intermediate levels such as the professionalization of medicine discussed in the previous chapter, in the end all of these patterns are emergent. They are patterns of individual, interpretive, rational action. So it is with the interpretive individual that we will have to begin. Parsons conceives of the pattern of social action emerging from sequences of unit acts strung together as courses of action. It is in the patterning of courses of action that social structure is to be found. Each course of action, then, is made up of moments identified as unit acts. The unit act is the foundation for all social life. In Parsons's view, there are four elements to the unit act:

(1) an actor;

(2) a situation made up of an environment of conditions;
(3) goals or ends to be achieved;
(4) a mode of orientation towards the elements in the unit act.

The mode of orientation gives the actor the grounds on which to define the situation and thus select appropriate means to attain the given ends. It is the mode of orientation which, in the theory, underpins the interpretive character of social action. Without it, social action would be indistinguishable from instinctive behaviour.

Since the primary characteristic of our social lives is that we live in the company of others, then one of the most important elements in the environment of surrounding conditions is the other. The other is conceived as another social actor standing in a situation and holding a mode of orientation. Both sides of the equation are now in place. How things will turn out can be affected from either side. Parsons calls this the double contingency. What the theory has to do is make the coordination of activities possible so that both actors can achieve the goals set. It is the purposeful character of social action which defines it. If the theory can provide for cooperation between the actors then it will make social order possible. A range of possibilities is available. One party could coerce the other into cooperation. The net result of this, in Parsons's view, would be enedemic hostility and the eventual break up of orderliness into a war of all against all. On the other hand, if we could so motivate actors that they would willingly comply with one another's expectations, then we would have a stable solution to the problem of order. In his theory, he achieves this motivated compliance by stipulating that social actors share a common culture. What they share are sentiments with regard to the ends which it is possible to achieve, expectations about how to achieve such ends and definitions of what actions and situations mean. If we begin by defining actors as sharing a common culture, then it is quite easy to make the next step and infer that each would define the other as engaged in reciprocal activities, complementary roles and the pursuit of rationally understandable courses of action. Putting it succinctly, Parsons solves the theoretical problem by presuming that actors see things in the same way and are predisposed to assume that the other will act in ways which they themselves would. The other is, for the social actor, a mirror image of themselves, that is a rational social actor. If we do attribute these characteristics to social actors then a solution to the problem of order is to hand. It is perfectly rational for me to get along with others and fall in with their plans of action because in so doing, and in general terms, I am able to achieve my goals all the more easily. In this way, the system of social action holds itself together and our social lives come to have the predictable, thoroughly routine nature that we generally know them to have. The top-down character of this account can be seen in the presumption of shared culture. The social character of individual actors is defined from the point of view of the culture. The culture is, itself, the defining characteristic of the system as a whole. It is what enables us to talk of groups of social actors making up a collectivity. Their membership of the collectivity is determined through the shared culture. Our interest in the activities of the members of this collectivity will be confined only to those aspects which display their possession of the common culture. To take a fairly obvious example, our interest in family life, say, will be in how families are organized through the allocation of roles and the legitimation of the sets of norms and values associated with them to reproduce the stable pattern of family life and hence to contribute towards the stability of the social structure as a whole.

We ought, at this point, to summarize what has been a very abbreviated discussion of Parsons's theory. First, Parsons defines social action in terms of means/ends rationality. Social actors are socialized, rational actors sharing a common culture. It is the participation in the common culture which enables mutual understanding to take place. On the basis of such understandings, definitions, roles, expectations and so forth are distributed. The coordination of social action is achieved by the performance of activities in accord with reciprocally defined and shared norms, or rules of behaviour.

Two elements, then, are central. One is the rationality of action defined in means/end terms. The other is mutual understanding. Garfinkel asks how we might engage in studies to make these visible. These two are entangled together for it is the assignment of a means/end rationality which gives some activity its sense. To bring out this entanglement, Garfinkel makes a move which we will find becoming more and more significant as we move through our discussion of his work and that of other ethnomethodologists. To make rationality and mutual understanding visible, we could proceed by dropping the presumption that both these characteristics are intrinsic to activities. That is to say, we could bracket the big assumption that when considered from the point of view of the theory, the things we do obviously and unproblematically make sense and are understandable. We should remember that dropping this assumption is a move we make within the theory and for theoretical purposes. We are not saying anything about how social life must be for ordinary social actors. We are exercising the theorist's prerogative to vary assumptions. Making such a move involves two steps. The assumption of shared meaning is set aside first for the actors themselves. We no longer presume a shared culture. Second, we drop the presumption of the community of observer and subject, i.e. the assumption that they automatically make sense to each other. The net result of the move is, then, that whatever sense we might then find activities to have would would have to have been produced for them.

This is not really a strange position for anthropologists and sociologists to adopt. They are quite used to making sense of activities which, on the surface at least, do not have any intrinsic meaning. Such sense is assigned to apparently meaningless acts by finding reasons for the actions to take place. More often than not, such reasons are latent functions of one kind or another. All that Garfinkel has done is to extend this process of finding or producing sense which anthropology takes to alien ways of life to the familiar and commonsense ones. After all, from the point of the theory, since the theorist knows nothing outside of the theory, there should be no difference between the familiar and the strange. In so doing he brings out the importance of what he calls lay sociological theorizing. The understandability and rationality of activities, and hence orderliness of social life, is the achievement of ordinary social actors, the outcome of what they do, and their commonsense knowledge of social structures just as the understandability and rationality of the rain dance is, for the professional sociologists, the outcome of his professional, scientific knowledge of social structures.

In the Parsonian framework, the rationality of action is underpinned by the shared rules and definitions encapsulated in the culture. But, because of the presumption of mutal understanding and rationality, the shared character of the rules is made invisible. To make it visible, we would have to search for occasions in which behaviour failed to conform to expectations and hence in which rules were breached. If we were able to set up encounters in which such failures were engineered, then, on the Parsonian theory, we ought to have rendered ordinary social life impossible. Breaking the expectations would mean it was no longer possible to define actions as rationally understandable. Any such actions would become specifically senseless, as Garfinkel puts it. We would not know how to treat them. This is precisely the point of the famous disruption experiments. Garfinkel devised these demonstrations as exercises for his students. They were designed to make visible and hence available for sociological reflection, the presupposition of mutual understanding which the Parsonian framework had taken for granted. Each of them takes a familiar setting and introduces a dimension of quite inappropriate behaviour. Counsellors answer questions randomly, acquaintances are interrogated minutely as to what they mean by commonplace remarks such as How are you?, and other endless searches for the meaning of behaviour are instituted. And yet, in the fact of this violation of the central tenet of Parsons's theory, social order does not collapse. To be sure, things do get uncomfortable. People do get huffy, offended, and so on. But the complete failure of mutual understanding does not occur. On Parsons's theory that is precisely what ought to have happened. Social order, it seems, is not as fragile and our grip on it as precarious as at least this sociologist might have us think.

The demonstrations have indicated a phenomenon which Parsons's presumption of a shared culture had caused to become invisible. The next task was to try to make that phenomenon amenable for study. Again, Garfinkels proceduralizing inclinations are at work. If what are shared by social actors are bodies of knowledge, lists of definitions and rules, then, at least in principle, it ought to be possible to specify the knowledge, rules and definitions so that the culture could be itemized and written out. Writing out a whole culture is, of course, not a practical task. But, given the view of culture as lists of rules and definitions, it ought to be possible to draw up the list for a defined and specified portion of the culture. This could be done by itemizing the meanings, for example, embedded in just one segment of a conversation. Garfinkel set his students to accomplish this task. Each student had to summarize a brief portion of a conversation and then explicate, clarify and elaborate what was said until all the meanings implicit in the conversation had been identified. The trouble was that the students found that as they proceeded the task became increasingly ramified. The more they wrote to clarify the original, the more they gave Garfinkel opportunities to find obscurities, vagueness and so on. Eventually, they gave up. They could not finish the task of specifying exactly what was meant, said, hinted, implied and so on. There was always more to say. Each gloss on the conversation became itself a resource for finding yet more meanings to elaborate. Table 3.1 shows an except from the exercise. The left-hand column is a comment made by a husband to his wife. The right-hand column is the first set of clarifications and elaborations.

These findings do not stand as a disproof of Parsons's theory. Not were they arrived at out of any attemp to test in this way. All that has been shown is that *if* we do share a common culture consisting of meanings, definitions and the like, then there is no way that on any occasion we can specify in so many words just what those meanings etc. might be. As we will see, this insight will become increasingly important as we develop enthnomethodo-logy's programme. But what of normative expectations? Surely here we are on firmer ground? Surely we can identify and list the range of behaviour which are relevant for some set of circumstances? To see if this was so, Garfinkel took one of the simplest possible scenarios, that of the two-person game tick-tack-toe (similar to noughts and crosses). Can the rules for this game be identified? Following what, in the previous chapter we saw were Felix Kaufman's suggestions concerning the rules of science, Garfin-kel suggests that any such rules might be either basic or definitional of the game or preferential. Preferential rules would define what is good, apt, sensible or accomplished play. Basic rules would define what was involved in playing at all. If one broke these rules, then whatever else one was doing,

Table 3.1

Husband:	Dana succeeded in putting a penny in a parking meter to-day without being picked up.	This afternoon as I was bringing Dana our four year old son home from the nursery school, he succeeded in reaching high enogh to put a penny in a parking meter when we were parked in a meter zone, whereas before he had always had to be picked up to reach that high… .

… As I progressively imposed accuracy, clarity, and distinctness, the task became increasingly laborious. Finally, when I required that they assume I would know what they had actually talked about only from reading literally what they wrote literally, they gave up with the complaint that the task was impossible.

(Garfinkel, *Studies in Ethnomethodology*, 1967, pp. 24–25)

one was no longer playing the game. Basic rules would provide, then what Garfinkel calls the game-furnished conditions of play. Breaking these should lead to play becoming specifically senseless.

Garfinkel tried to break the basic rules of tic-tac-toe by rubbing his opponent's mark out, by putting more than one mark at a time in, by placing his mark on the intersection of cells, and so on. But while his actions caused no little confusion, and even anger at times, they did not bring about the breakdown of social interaction. Instead, players seemed to have a variety of ways of dealing with the puzzles which Garfinkel set them. In some cases, there seemed to be a strategy of wait and see. Although at the time it looked as if it was impossible to make sense of what was going on, players seemed to expect that in time all would become clear. Earlier puzzles would be resolved by later explanations and revelations. No attempt was made to fit every case to its own rule. Rules were extended, suppressed, and ignored on what appeared to be an *ad hoc* basis. Most importantly, if the behaviour in hand did not appear to affect anything in a material way, then things were allowed to run their course. In the face of

the attempted breaches of trust and expectations, what Durkheim identified as the moral order of daily life exerts such a powerful presence that
considerable lengths will be gone to in order to retain, if at all possible, the
things-as-usual character of ordinary life.

Garfinkel's attempts to proceduralize Parsons's theory, to develop
studies which would enable us to specify precisely and definitively what
elements a common culture had, failed. The task he had set himself proved
intractable. The only way forward, or so it seemed, was to suspend the
assumption of a shared culture, and with it the means/end rationality of
action. We have already seen that making the first move involves treating
the rationality and understandability of action as an outcome of what
people do and not a given premiss for it. Making the latter as well, involves
stepping back beyond the premisses which Parsons had set himself. What
Parsons took for granted will have now to be scrutinized. Whatever
character activities have, their rationality, sense, understandability (what
Garfinkel calls their accountability), must be treated as the outcome of
those actions, their accomplishment. The achievement of rationality,
understandibility and so on takes place in and through the performance of
the actions themselves. To use a term which we will take up at length in the
next chapter, the accountability of action is reflexive.

If we suspend the presumption of a common culture, what can we equip
our social actors with? More importantly, what do we *have to* equip them
with? These are the next questions. If we set aside the assumption of a
shared culture, *somehow* social actors have to display the knowledge and
understanding which they have. The procedural task is to specify just how
they do it. And, what is more, to specify how they do it in systematic,
methodical, routine ways. The name which Garfinkel gave the investigation of these methods was ethnomethodology. The explanation why he
called it this is quite simple. For some time, anthropologists and others had
been studying the classifications and practices which many different societies have to solve the problems we solve through our institutions of science,
medicine and so forth. The studies of these classifications and practices
were called ethnomedicine, ethnobotany etc. and what they were primarily
concerned with was the organization of the knowledge which ordinary
members of the societies in question had about how to cure diseases, what
sorts of plants were to be found in the neighbouring area, and so on. If one
wanted a name for the study of the methods which ordinary people in a
society have for making their knowledge and understandings available,
then why not call it ethnomethodology?

We ought, at this point, to re-emphasize an important feature of
Garfinkel's distinctive stance. In suspending the presumption of a shared
culture, we are taking two important steps. First, the commonality of

meanings is no longer taken for granted by the theory. Second, such commonality is no longer posited for actors. If such mutual understandings are achieved then they are based upon an establishment of a common definition of the situation. In the next chapters, our discussion of Garfinkel, Wieder and others, will take up the question of how, in actual cases, social actors may be said to achieve it. The net result is to make social actors inquirers into the accountability of actions. As we hinted just now, one of the most important premises of ethnomethodology is that both common sense and scientific reasoning involve the interpretation of social structures and that, therefore, the distinction is not between sociologists and others, but between two kinds of sociological investigator, lay and professional ones. The difference between them is not in terms of whether they treat the organization of social scenes as matters of inquiry, but in the attitudes which govern their inquiries: lay sociologists investigate the social setting from within the natural attitude and out of a concern with practicality, while professional ones approach it from the standpoint of the theoretical attitude. We can talk about lay social theory because, as inquirers into the accountability of actions, ordinary people call upon sets of classifications of persons and activities, accounts of the connections between actions, and so on.

Once we start to think about the problems of operationalizing the presumptions, several problems come to the fore. How can we make these methodical procedures visible? No help can be obtained from within the Parsonian framework because the rational conception of action and the commonality of culture are its presuppositions. There is no way to step back beyond them and remain within the framework. There is one possibility, though. At the heart of the scheme is a notion of voluntarism. This is, as we mentioned, derived from Weber. We would seek out alternative approaches to this voluntarism, other ways of founding interpretive sociology which do not begin with common knowledge but with shared experience. It was precisely this which Alfred Schutz set out to do. He sought a set of concepts which would put interpretive sociology on as firm a grounding as possible. Such concepts all relate to what Schutz was to call the intersubjective character of social life. Garfinkel uses the notion of intersubjectivity to radicalize Parsons. By means of it, he steps back beyond the premiss of shared understanding.

Before we begin to explore the detail, we ought to see what turning to Schutz in this way might mean. The first thing to say is that Schutz cannot simply be added to Parsons to fill out, supplement or complement to latters views. Garfinkel is not Parsons plus Schutz. Each of these theorists premissed their work in entirely different traditions. Part of the differences between them can be seen in the attitudes which they hold to the vary activity of theorizing itself. The choices which are made at this primitive level precede sociological theorizing and investigations themselves and are not resolved by the outcomes of such theorizing or by calling into play the findings those investigations yield. In radicalizing Parsons, Garfinkel gave up a deeply entrenched sociological tradition which is shared not simply by conventional theorists like Durkheim and Weber, but by American behaviourism as well. In taking up Schutz, he took on board an entirely different one. The importance of the choices might appear in two different but not necessarily unrelated guises. It might matter which choice we made if we felt that the most pressing problem for the social sciences was the provision of a secure philosophical foundation. Such a foundation might consist in a set of indubitable propositions, for example, or a set of rules for transporting sociological propositions into psychological ones, etc. etc. Given the interests we have sketched out, such a problem might be defined as laying out the foundations of an interpretive sociology. This is a theorist's worry, and is precisely what occupied both Parsons and Schutz throughout their lives. As we can see from the letters they sent to one another, they were profoundly at odds on how to set about this. Parsons was committed to a version of Kantian philosophy which he calls analytic realism. Our knowledge of the world, both natural and social, is not simply the product of our experience. It is also a consequence of our reason. Scientifically rational understanding must be premissed in sets of categories which, in reason, we cannot doubt. These categories tell us how things must be for us to be able to experience them at all. The systematic use of these categories in defined ways in science enable us to have knowledge which is independent of anyones particular, subjective experience. Such systematic use is set out in the rules and procedures of scientific method. Parsons's scheme of levels of action (internality/externality) and modes of orienation (instrumentation/expressivism) is an attempt to give sociology a set of categories similar to those available for the natural sciences.

The tradition which Schutz worked within, phenomenology, rejected this idea. As we have already indicated in our introduction, Husserl felt that it was possible to reach back to the foundation of all experience through the use of his phenomenological method. This foundation, what he calls pure experience, undergirds science just as much as it does commonsense knowledge of the world. This pure experience constitutes the apodictic evidence on which a truly rigorous science could be based. It is the task of phenomenology to describe this stratum of pure experience. The method for arriving at these descriptions involves bracketing, or suspending judgement on the property under scrutiny, be it length, colour, hardness, reality, truth or rationality, to see how the organization of our experience of objects constitutes their reality, truth, colour, hardness or rationality. Such organizing can be seen when we reflect upon the different attitudes which we adopt towards the phenomena of experience. For Kant, and for Parsons, it is categories and concepts which must have priority, For Schutz and Husserl it is the phenomena of experience. This is what is summarized in the slogan we have already mentioned: To the things themselves!

The securing of firm philosophical foundations is one way that these pre-sociological choices might be important. For some like Garfinkel, concerned largely with procedural and operational matters, they take on a different hue. The question over which Husserl and Kant are in disagreement is not one on which sociology is competent *qua sociology* to comment. Neither can sociological investigations and theories help to resolve the problem. But, the very fact that there is such deep disagreement poses a puzzle. If such choices of philosophical foundations are available, which should be adopted? This is particularly acute if, as seems to be the case here, both satisfy the canons of systematicity, rigour and so on which we identified in the previous chapter. In such circumstances, the only reasonable way to make a choice is in terms of the possibilities which the choices offer the sociologist. Part of Garfinkel's operationalizing endeavour, then, is to see just which possibilities Schutz and Husserl are making available. In particular, do they offer the possibility of following the animal in ways that Kant and Parsons do not?

Once again, we have run very quickly through what is a very complex argument and have staked everything on a single claim. A great deal more could be said about the pre-theoretical elections which Parsons and Schutz make and of the ways in which they are explored by Garfinkel. However, were we to take up these matters here in the detail required to do them full justice, we would far overrun our allotted space. Those who wish to pursue these matters more closely are advised to consult the readings which we have listed.

Following Husserl's lead, Schutz took the pivot of his theorizing to be the experience of the individual. The theory is constructed so that the experiencing subject is central. From the point of view of any such individual, the world which is experienced is *my* world. It is the world as it appears to me. An approach which puts this conception of experience at the forefront of theorizing is egological. The topic to be investigated is the nature of the experiences of the experiencing individual. To achieve this, the theory will have to bracket or reduce the phenomena of the familiar world of daily life until that stratum of pure experience is reached from which no further reduction can be made. The theory will then have reached the essence of experience. This *eidos* is the ground of all experience. In developing his interpretive sociology, Schutz brings out an important theme to be found in the later work of Husserl, namely the constitution of the lifeworld. In the lifeworld of daily life, we experience objects, people, theories and so on, in ways that are very different to those in which we experience them in science, for example. In the lifeworld we adopt the natural attitude. In science we find the theoretical attitude displayed. What characterizes the natural attitude is the presumption that things are as they appear. We do not suppose that for our ordinary purposes our senses will play tricks upon us or will need to be supplemented, extended or improved. Neither do we suppose that our theoretical expressions will be inconstant need of check, validation, or revision. We take the way things appear to be the fact of the matter; our theories and accounts stand without scrutiny until further notice. None of these things hold for the scientific attitude. There nothing is beyond scrutiny and revision; there appearances can be taken to be deceptive, misleading, even erroneous. Our senses are in constant need of supplementation, if not outright replacement. We believe what the instruments tell us, what the formula gives us, rather than our eyes and ears. Schutz himself did not investigate the foundations of mathematics and science (although Husserl did) and concentrated on the presuppositions of the lifeworld. Just what is it we take for granted in daily life and how do these presuppositions organize our mundane experience? In his studies, he found that he could not accept all of Husserl's ideas, particularly those associated with the possibility of a realm of pure experience.

For the experiencing individual, the experience of the world is not an unending stream of undifferentiated sensual stimuli. Experience in the lifeworld, what Schutz following Bergson call the *duree*, is organised. We experience objects, people, events. This organization if facilitated by what Schutz and Husserl call the *epoche of the natural attitude*. We said just now that what characterizes the scientific attitude is that anything can be doubted. Even the most basic propositions are available for scrutiny and revision. In the natural attitude, this possibility is suspended. Instead a policy of refraining from doubt is adopted. Following the dictates of this policy, the possibility of doubting, for instance, that things are not as they seem is set to one side. The world of daily life, the world of ordinary experience, is taken by us to be primordially the real world. Things just are as they appear.

The real social world is taken to be an intersubjective one. We share it with other experiencing subjects. These other subjects with whom I interact are taken by me to have a reciprocity of perspectives with me. If they stood where I stand, knowing just what I do, they would see things as I do. If they were to do this, they would share my interests and relevances. It follows from this that they would act exactly as I would. And vice versa. This latter point cannot be overemphasized. It is this postulate or presupposition which underwrites the essential character of daily life. Since I presume others would see things as I do and would act as I do, then I presume mutual understandability. In the world of intersubjective beings, I can make myself understood. Such a possibility is only available because of the possibilities inherent in the reciprocity of perspectives. It is crucial to see that Schutz is describing the natural attitude here, not mounting a philosophical argument for its veracity, logicality, indubitability etc. He is describing the very foundations of social life.

The intersubjective world does not appear to us as our creation. It appears pre-given for us and as having a factual status independent of us. The real world is already there and we find ourselves in its midst. But, although that factual status is independent of us, it is nonetheless the outcome of our taking it for granted. We do not doubt the worlds factual character. This is, perhaps what should be meant by that much abused and misused phrase the social construction of reality. The factuality of the world is given in its continuity over time. These other subjects with whom we interact are predecessors, contemporaries and successors. Alongside the postulate of temporal continuity are two further ones concerning the bodies or stocks of knowledge available to the subject. One of these postulates is that any experience is not purely unique. Experiences will continue in the future much as they have in the past. Schutz calls this the 'and so forth' assumption. Second, there is the assumption that, given the same circumstances, I can do it again. No action is unique.

These postulates organize the stream of experience in the *duree*. Schutz's sociology explores them in detail. The lifeworld we share, the perspectives which we hold, are seen as so many discrete modes of acting and being, what he calls finite provinces of meaning. Within each of these provinces, distinctive understandings and interpretations are made. Schutz contrasts the wide-awakeness of ordinary life with dreams, the theatre, fiction and fantasy. In each of these, the reality of the experience is constituted differently. The reality of the stage is not the reality of daily life. These finite provinces of meaning are structured both by their own relevances and by the nature of time within them. In our ordinary day-to-day affairs time is a continuous flow. In dreams we go back and forth, as we do in novels, the cinema and so on. Similarly, what we know of others is organized within finite provinces of meaning into types. We have typical heroes and typical villains in novels; we have typical motorists and typical shopkeepers in daily life. Our experience within such finite provinces of meaning and our movement between them is one continuous flow of action. Yet, at the level of inner time consciousness, in daydreams, time may slow down or speed up, just as it may when we are concentrating wholeheartedly on the task in hand.

From the point of view which Schutz elaborates, the problem which

Parsons sets up for sociology has to be recast. Instead of motivated compliance, what has to be investigated are the ways by which the recognizability of a finite province of meaning is displayed and shared through common experience and shared knowledge within the flow of that experience and without knowing in advance just what knowledge is to be relevant. Making finite provinces of meaning observable, recognizable and so shareable is the reproduction of social life as the mundane, no-problem affair that, most of the time, it is for all of us. This achievement is what practical reasoning accomplishes.

Notice what has happened. Under Schutz's rubric, what any finite province of meaning might be, what any action is, what it means, is treated as a matter for investigation and display by social actors. The accountability of action, its place in the social structure, must be made visible. We can now draw out the contrast with Parsons in an explicit way. For Parsons the prime question is the systemic resolution of the double contingency, that is how actors reproduce the systemic character of their activities as they go along. For Schutz, it is the achievement of a shared finite province of meaning and its maintenance in an through our shared common experience. For the double contingency to be a problem, first there has to be a shared definition of the situation. Investigating how this is achieved is what Schutz means by radicalizing Parsons. Garfinkel takes up this project and seeks to demonstrate how it might be achieved in what he calls his study policies. These can be summarized as a set of investigative maxims such as the following:

(1) treat activities as reflexively accountable;
(2) treat settings as self-organizing and commonsense as an occasioned corpus of knowledge;
(3) treat social actors as inquirers into those settings and accounts.

Utilizing these maxims, it becomes possible to investigate social settings to see how their essential character, their factuality, is accomplished. In the next chapter we will show how Garfinkel does this.

4

Implementing the programme

METHODOLOGICAL TROUBLES

The arguments in the previous chapter indicate that the relationship between theories and investigations is conceived rather differently in ethnomethodology than it is in sociology generally. There, the building of theories is typically regarded as the primary task and the construction of a comprehensive sociological theory as the end of the whole exercise. The making of studies is obviously important to this, but it has a subsidiary role in the enterprise, and the problems of research are residual. Thus, the assumption is that once the theoretical problems of sociology are solved, then the difficulties in making investigations will be relatively easily dealt with. The conception we have been developing gives a very different and much more prominent place to studies: we have treated theories as means toward making investigations. The question of what it takes to make successful investigations is not residual to but critical for the formulation of theories. The conduct of studies, further, provides a powerful constraint on theorizing, for the studies show the properties of phenomena with which theorizing must come to terms. From ethnomethodology's point of view, there ceases to be much point in asking what the tasks of sociological theory are in a general way, without reference to particular problems, phenomena and specific research materials.

That there is a gap between sociological theory and research is something which is regularly complained about by sociologists themselves. Since we have been using the example of Parsons, we can point to the way in which, in the 1950s Parsons was chastised for engaging in grand theory, the kind that was so comprehensive that it became almost vapid. Grand theory would not do, people could not see how the abstractions of the theory ever came to talk about recognizable things. It was felt, then, that a different kind of theory was called for. Thus, for example, Robert Merton, whose outlook otherwise had much in common with that of Parsons, proposed that theories of the middle range were called for. These were less ambitious than Parsons grandiose schemes and hence would be much more closely related to recognizable topics and much more easily linked to the findings of research. As we say, the gap between theory and research is well enough known about, and ways of overcoming it are regularly proposed, though many of these involve proposing a different kind of theory. Ethnomethodology, too, sees a gap between theory and research but instead of thinking that the answer is to be found in contriving a different kind of theory, it offers different way of reconstructing the situation: research and theorizing are to be done in conjunction, such that the theorizing is tied to the materials generated by the research.

If the gap between theory and research is well known and openly debated between sociologists then the gap between research and phenomena is equally well known but far less well aired. This is, to ethnomethodology, just as important as the gap between theory and research, because the relationship really involves three elements: theory, research and phenomenon. The materials generated by research provide the objects of theorizing because, supposedly, they exhibit the properties of the phenomena that the theory is intended to understand. However, it is well known to sociological researchers that their methods do not enable them to capture the properties of phenomena. The results of sociological studies are invariably debatable and they are almost universally open to objection on methodological grounds. For example, the measurement procedures which sociologists use often measure, if they measure anything at all, something other than they are supposed to. Garfinkel, for example devotes a long discussion to the re-examination of quantitative studies of admissions to psychiatric treatment which are designed to identify the selection criteria involved in order to show that these studies, at the very least, are often describing things other than they propose to be describing. Sociologists have trouble in getting access, through their methods, to the phenomena they aim to study.

The phenomenological influence encourages ethnomethodology to put faithfulness to the phenomenon before anything else. If one aims to look clearly, and without prejudice at the phenomenon then one seeks to describe as accurately as one can what one sees. It is the appearance of the phenomenon which is to dictate what is reported, not *any* preconceptions about how things should be reported and described. Here is a deep difference between ethnomethodologists and others. The latter are apt to think that there are rules which should dictate how description is done, that there are rules of scientific inquiry which require that descriptions of phenomena should take a certain form. The conception that they have is very often one that involves the idea that things should be described in quantitative terms, for example. These conceptions are typically derived from the philosophy of science, or from other ideas of how things are in the natural sciences. That these ideas are often derived from positivist philosophies is not the issue. The issue is, rather, that these ideas are *derived*, they are taken up before and set the conditions for the description of the phenomena, and this means that, if we attempt to follow them through, we begin by looking at the phenomena *through* a grid that we have imposed upon it. Whatever justification and value there might be for doing that, it obviously does not fit with the phenomenologically-inspired idea of looking at the phenomena independently of all those pre-conceptions we can possibly dispense with and especially those provided by taking over methods developed for purposes other than our own. Descriptions are not to be constrained by some pre-given conception of the form description ought to take but, instead, by whatever considerations are necessary to portray the phenomena as exactly as we can. This can be taken as an encouragement to methodological laxity, but it certainly is not intended as that. Far from inciting investigators to carry on in any undisciplined way they please, it is meant to impose a most stringent discipline, but one which originates with the phenomenon rather than in some set of received rules. The description is supposed to develop from the most careful observation of the phenomenon and to report what was observed as meticulously as that can be done.

Since the methods routinely employed in sociology are contrived according to preconceived notions of how an objective study ought to be done, and since those methods persistently fail to identify the properties of social phenomena in the way that they do, then the possibility arises that the problems of research are inherent in the methodological programme. It may be that the methods, far from exposing the properties of phenomena are obscuring these from view, that the attempt is being made to handle phenomena in terms of a methodological apparatus that is incongruous to them. The treatment of this as a serious possibility would involve the adoption of very different attitudes.

Let us repeat, there is much agreement amongst sociologists that studies currently fail to identify the things they are supposed to measure or otherwise describe. Let us add that ethnomethodologists and other sociologists are also often in agreement as to why such difficulties plague inquiries.

Take, for example, the fact that the affairs of everyday life are frequently conducted in ordinary language. The business of sociological inquiry is, from many peoples point of view, desirably conducted in mathematical terms, but expression in ordinary language is very difficult to characterize mathematically. It cannot be assumed that there is the necessary isomorphism between respective structures of mathematics and ordinary language if the former is to be used to describe the other. Such, in essence, is Cicourel's key argument, in his *Method and Measurement* about much mathematical and quantitative thinking in sociology. One of the reasons why ordinary language does not lend itself to description in mathematical terms is because of its indexical character.

Since ethnomethodology is difficult to understand, it is tempting to seize on some of the things which seem clearest as if these give a key to its understanding. Two terms seem to stand out in Garfinkel's *Studies* and these have been latched on to as though they were its distinctive and crucial concepts. These are the expressions indexical and reflexive (and we shall say something about the latter later.) However, the notion that the expressions of ordinary language are indexical did not originate with Garfinkel at all. He takes up the fact of the indexical character of ordinary language because it is such a well known fact amongst those interested in language. Much of the concern with indexical expressions originates with logicians, because such expressions create real troubles for the formulation of abstract forms of valid inference, which is, of course, logician's business. Indexical expressions are those which depend for their sense upon the circumstances of their production, of who said them, when, where, in relation to what and so forth. Leading examples of indexicals are such as 'this' or 'here' for in order to know what somebody is talking about when they say 'this' or which location is covered by 'here' one needs to know something about the local circumstances of the speech, what the speaker is pointing at, where he is standing etc. Garfinkel does not *introduce* the notion of indexical but proposes a different attitude toward indexical expressions than is usually taken.

From the viewpoint of logicians, indexical expressions are looked upon as a nuisance, a problem for those who want to formulate general statements or formulae that will be true without regard for the circumstances under which they are uttered. The thing to do, they therefore think (and many sociologists take the same view), is to eradicate indexical expressions and replace them by objective ones throughout. They find, however, that when they set out to do this, it is more than a bit difficult, and there is, to use Garfinkel's own words, an unsatisfied programmatic distinction between and substitutability of objective for indexical expressions. (*Studies in Ethnomethodology*, 1967, p.4) It is, that is, easy enough to propose that there are two kinds of expression, objective and indexical, but it is more than problematical to say which expressions are which and to achieve the kind of systematic substitution of one for the other that is intended. The fact that indexical expressions are disapproved of and yet are so difficult to eradicate makes them doubly troublesome. Garfinkel proposes a change in attitude, pointing out that indexical expressions are not a nuisance in the context of ordinary discourse, for such discourse goes about its orderly way *through* the use of such expressions. Everyday discourse has a plain sense which the users have no difficulty in grasping. Their exchanges, rather than suffering from, actually *depend upon* the indexical nature of expressions, and it is through a grasp of the circumstances of an utterance that persons are able to assign it a definite sense. Rather than criticize ordinary language because it falls short of someone's methodological ideals, Garfinkel intends to study it, treating its indexical character as one of its leading features and seeking to see how the users of ordinary language routinely and unremarkably make sense of indexical expressions.

There is, then, much agreement amongst ethnomethodologists and other sociologists that, *from the vantage point of conventional conceptions and practices of methods*, indexical expressions are a sore trouble and their pervasive presence in ordinary language makes rigorous research more than a little difficult. The difference between them (very often) is not over what the problems are or how they originate, but what to do about them. Are these problems ones that are contingent to or inherent in the standard conception of method? Is the thing to do to persist with that conception, or to give it up and adopt an entirely different one? The answer to the second question is, of course, likely to be much dependent on the answer to the first.

One way of looking at these problems is as nuisances. Yes, there are shortcomings of the methods, but we are broadly on the right lines and if we stick at it, develop and sophisticate our line of approach then we will eventually overcome them. There is another way though. These problems are persistent, and there is little progress in dealing with them. They turn up over and over again, and ways of facing up to them in one study by no means provide a general solution to them; other people making similar studies will have to deal with these problems all over again for themselves. There is something fundamentally wrong with the line of approach, the problems are inherent in the methods themselves, and the ways in which research is set up reproduces the very problems it discovers. The most dedicated persistence and ingenuity within that conception is not going to produce a solution. None can be had in those terms. This latter possibility is certainly not inconceivable to ethnomethodology.

We are not trying to say it is obviously right to choose ethnomethodology's conclusion. We want only to establish that the options are pretty much symmetrical, that there is just as much reason to think that a wholly new approach may pay off better than persisting with the old one.

The availability of these options does mean a parting of the ways between those who want to go on in much the same way and those who want to try going at things in an altogether different fashion.

Take the vexed question of common sense.

Felix Kaufmann, whose codification of the rules of science we mentioned in Chapter 2, points out that science knows only that which has admitted to the body of its findings by the appropriate procedures. Kaufmann was trying to identify widely held views about science and in this case he identified, we think, one which many sociologists would accept. It provides them with the basis for the criticism of common sense. What people in society say they know has not been acquired by the approved methods which qualify it for inclusion amongst the things science takes as known. A scientist should take at least a moderately sceptical attitude to any item of popular belief until it has been tested against suitably scientific standards. Science does not depend upon common sense, but must be independent of it.

Note, however, the upshot of Kaufmann's thoughts for a discipline like sociology which is setting itself up, rather than established. Since the discipline has no established and agreed standards for inclusion within the corpus of knowledge, nor anything acquired according to those standards the the theorist, *qua theorist,* knows nothing. His inquiries will determine the nature of the phenomena, but since he has not yet made those inquiries he does not know what that nature will prove to be. Yet sociologists argue about how sociology is to be done if it is to be adequate, and in doing so they appeal to what they already know about how real social structures are organized. They cannot, however, know this on the strength of the science's inquiries since this knowledge is being appealed to in order to define the science's proper forms of inquiry. Hence, they must possess this knowledge by something other than conformity to the rules of scientific inquiry. They often hold it by virtue of their membership in society and are appealing, therefore, to what anyone knows or can find out just by living in the society. In other words, to that which is common sense and obvious.

If one thinks it desirable for sociology to be independent of common sense one may see dependence on it as a regrettable necessity in the short run. Common-sense assumptions may be made and needed to get the show on the road but once it is moving, one can bring up those assumptions for examination and, if need be, dispense with them, achieving the progressive elimination of reliance on common sense. Is it, however, possible to achieve this, or is recourse to common-sense understandings something which, in sociological inquiries, is unavoidable?

One place where this question becomes acute is in the coding and analysis of survey data. The data consist of the answers to questions which have to be turned into uniform, consistent categories by some sort of coding procedure. Attempts are made to make coding an explicit, step-by-step procedure which is carried on in a standard, virtually mechanical way, by each practitioner. It should, ideally, involve the working out of an algorithm which spells out, at each point, the steps which the researcher is to take, and specifies how he is to choose between alternative possibilities and how to handle any eventuality that arises. A set of coding rules seems one way to ensure that coding is done in the desirable manner, rules which tell the coders just what they are to do.

How, in reality, do people go about the work of coding? Coders are supposed to act in ways which can be called faithfully following coding instructions. The point is not to make an exposé of coding by arguing that the coders often violate coding instructions and make no effort to follow them faithfully. This certainly is sometimes true and may be very common, but the point is to draw attention to what is done *when the coders are doing their level best to stick faithfully to the instructions*. The argument is: the coders have unavoidably to deviate from the coding instructions in order to follow them through, to satisfy themselves and others that they have actually and rightly done what they were supposed to. They will be compelled, for example, to abandon the letter of the instructions in order to comply with their spirit.

Just what the coders will have to do in order to get the coding done is not something that anyone can definitely say in advance. Though coding instructions are written out, they will be used very much in a wait and see fashion. Whether the coding instructions will actually work is something that will be discovered as the coding work gets under way and as problems arise. It will be found, for example, that coding instructions as written out prove to be ambiguous or unclear, though they may have seemed unequivocal when first composed, and that they will have to be rewritten. Those doing the coding will find that, far from providing them with exhaustive instructions on what to do in any and every eventuality, the instructions will often leave them at a loss. However, they will also appreciate that those who compile the instructions do not want to be constantly approached for answers to particular questions and guidance on particular problems and so those doing the coding will decide for themselves what they should do in actual instances. The work of coding will get done, and it will get done in ways which satisfy the parties to it that a proper job has been done, though no one can say exactly what was done in order to achieve this. The coders will have done as well as they, as anyone, *realistically* could, indeed they will have done the only things they could if the work was to be done at all. The work will have involved the coders in making lots of decisions about how the coding instructions are to be applied, to use their good sense to decide what the right thing was to do in situations of doubt and so on, settling for themselves what, here, now, is necessary to follow the instructions as faithfully as one can.

In order that the reader may see what is being talked about more clearly through some illustration, consider the following case. In a Canadian study of people's leisure time and domestic activities, questions were asked about what people did in the evening and where they did those things. Categories of response in terms of the location of the activities were provided for: did they do them in the bathroom, the living room, bedroom, yard, garden and so forth? One answer gave a real problem, because the respondent was recorded on the schedule to be coded as having said that he and his wife sat out in the evenings in their garden. This puzzled the coders because in Canada, 'garden' is used for the area in which things are grown and in contrast to yard which is a lawn like area in which games are played or where people might sit out. The answer is to be coded, but how? Assuredly those doing the coding are not going to return to the respondent to ask him the question again, or to get him to clarify his remarks: that would take altogether too much trouble and slow up the work. No, they are going to figure out how to code the answer for themselves. They can do that, by recognizing that English people use the word garden differently than do Canadians, and that English people use the word garden to include what Canadians would call the yard. Thus, the coders can check that the respondents are of English origin and be satisfied that what they *must have meant to say* in the terms of the coding schedule is that in the evenings they sit out in their yard. They could not have been saying that they did something unreasonable like sitting out in the middle of their vegetable patch but must have been saying something quite reasonable, and given what is known about the difference between English and Canadian speakers, this must have been it.

This example is given to show the unobtrusive but persistent reliance that the work of coding must have upon the fact that those who are to do it, if they are to be able to decide how things are to be correctly coded, are able to find their way around the society, are possessed of a practical knowledge of how people in it talk and act. It is not intended to question the validity of the survey study or even the correctness of the conclusion in the particular case, but to highlight the way in which, for deciding *what really happened* and *what was really said* in actual cases people must appeal to or at least imagine the actual circumstances of what was done and said. Insofar as one can claim, then, that the coded results correspond to the real facts they are meant to record, then that claim depends upon the use of coders common-sense judgements to decide what must really have happened and how that is properly to be coded. The coding instructions can work as well as they do *because of* not despite a reliance upon common-sense understandings.

Garfinkel maintains that reliance upon common sense knowledge of social structures is an indispensable feature of sociological inquiry, since it is a condition of being able to say, in any actual instance, what definitely happened. In this, he echoes Schutz and Husserl on the lifeworld and science. Hence, any researcher collecting data which is intended to comprise a record of what people really did must invoke, in order to close off uncertainty and equivocality, their common-sense understanding of how things can possibly be (as the coders invoked their knowledge that reasonable people just do not sit in the vegetable patch). He does many things which are designed to amplify, document and show the implications of this claim. Two can be mentioned.

The first involves one of the notorious experiments, that of getting people to behave like lodgers in their own homes and to describe what transpires there as though written from the point of view of the lodger. After all, in terms of many conceptions of method, the lodger would be thought to be more like the objective scientific observer than would any member of the family. The lodger is not a party to the household, he is a stranger to it who knows nothing of the history, details and understandings obtaining amongst its members and is therefore witnessing only that which occurs before his eyes, without making gratuitous inferences about what goes on. However, the consequence of attempting to look at a social scene through the eyes of a stranger was not that people felt that they had got a better, more accurate and objective view of what was happening, but that this view could not capture the actualities of what was taking place. Seeing what was really going on amongst the members of the family involved knowing a lot about them, their relationships, past histories and so forth.

More formally, Garfinkel has argued that the use of a documentary method is an indispensable feature of factual reasoning about social action, and that this makes the use of common-sense knowledge inescapable.

FINDING AN OBJECTIVE SOCIAL STRUCTURE

The notion of documentary method is one which Garfinkel takes over from Karl Mannheim. It is not to be thought of as identifying some specialized method of sociological inquiry, comparable to fieldwork, the survey and so forth, and certainly is not to be thought to be about a method which makes use of written documents. It is, rather, meant to single out a particular form of reasoning in which particular things are used to show or demonstrate the existence of an underlying pattern (i.e. to document, or evidence the presence of the pattern.) Since, to put it most crudely, sociological analysis is aimed at discovering the underlying pattern, the underlying social structure, which is present in the particular and observable activities of members of society, then this kind of reasoning is its stock in trade.

Popular sociological opinion to the contrary, ethnomethodology does not contradict Durkheim's famous proposal that we should treat social facts as things, that we should recognize social structures as external and objective, environments capable of constraining our conduct. *Nobody* supposes that anyone can do anything they like, that anyone can act as they will regardless of the limits that the world sets upon them. Nobody supposes that or anything like it. However, without contradicting Durkheim's slogans it is possible to see different significances in them than sociologists have usually done. One is not compelled to ask, as the next question, *how do social structures operate as causal determinants of individual action?* This is the question that Durkheim himself saw as being more prominently posed by his slogans, and even those sociologists who do not agree with Durkheim on other things have tended to accept his terms for subsequent argument. For example, many interactionists have wanted to deny that social structures are causal determinants of action, but in doing so accept that the issue is whether or not social structures are causal determinants. Ethnomethodology's interest in Durkheim's slogan is rather different and results in the issues being located in quite another place. Thus the argument that ethnomethodology is a version of symbolic interactionism is a misrepresentation.

Durkheim wants to argue a little more than that social structures are objective. He wants to argue that they are *visibly* objective. It is, for Durkheim, a matter of fact that anyone can see, in the scenes of daily life the presence of an objective social structure. Durkheim can support his contentions about the objectivity of social structures by mentioning familiar and everyday occurrences. For example, we all know that if we break the law then society will take restraining action against us, it will prevent us from acting and may even destroy us. Society's objectivity is, then, if Durkheim's argument is followed out, something that is known from within the society. It is a routinely encountered feature of life in the society. And that brings us back, of course, to the topic of *the world of daily life as we experience it.* It is a primordial feature of the world as experienced that it is experienced as objective: Schutz's analysis assumes the fact that we find ourselves in the social world, that it is already there for us. The question that ethnomethodology finds in Durkheim's slogans, then, is: how are objective social structures made visible? Another way of asking it is: how does a social structure acquire its visible, demonstrable objectivity?

Note one further aspect of out interpretation of what Durkheim's arguments mean: social structures are visibly objective to both members of the society and professional sociological inquirers, and one may therefore ask ethnomethodology's questions quite indifferently of both those who just live in the society and those who make their profession out of studying it. Since those who just live within the society have to detect, discover and recognize that objectivity, to ask how they do so is to treat them, as the study policy recommends, as inquirers themselves, people who are involved—as a part of their practical lives—in finding out about social structures.

In order to make the next few points, let us do so through an example, which uses a study which deals with a phenomenon which would stand as a classic Durkheiman social fact. It is the convict code, and we depend for this account on D. Lawrence Wieders study of it (*Language and Social Reality*, 1974) Wieder was not the first to undertake a study of it. Others had already done so, and they had found that the lives of convicts were governed by a regular pattern, that the same pattern of behaviour would be present amongst groups of convicts even though the personnel in the groups were wholly different. The convict code was a Durkheimian social fact in the sense that it was a *moral* order, a set of rules for proper behaviour which governed the lives of convicts and which remained unchanged over time and despite changes in the personnel acting it out. It was binding on the lives of convicts and those who violated it would be punished. The code, as far as those who live under its auspices and also those who have dealings with convicts and ex-convicts are concerned is an unquestionable reality, an indubitable fact of life. If one is dealing with convicts, then the existence of the code is something that one must take into account, recognize what it will and will not allow convicts to do. The code is objective alright, experienced as such and treated as an inescapable fact of life. It is this kind of thing that studies of convict life reveal.

It is at this point that many sociological arguments begin. Does the code explain the behaviour of the convicts? Such an argument is likely to be a specific form of the more general debate about what kinds of things can explain human actions. Can rules do this? Rules are a kind of idea, and there is an open question as to whether ideas can really explain actions. Put another way, rules, as a kind of idea, are properly counted as part of culture, and the question then is: does culture rather than structure (i.e. the arrangement of social relations) determine what people do?

Which side is ethnomethodology to take on these questions? Many think that it opts for the idealist side and for a kind of cultural determinism but that presupposes that ethnomethodology is trying to get into the business of explanation. The interest of phenomenology is in description, rather than explanation, and ethnomethodology pursues descriptive, rather than explanatory aims. It goes, therefore, rather further back than the starting point of the controversies just mentioned and notes that the questions about whether rules can adequately explain the pattern of conduct presupposes that both the patterns of conduct and the relevant rules have been identified and described. It furthermore assumes that whether or not the rules do have an explanatory connection with the actions making up the pattern that they do have another, more basic connection with them, i.e. that they are *rules for that setting*. The convict code is identified by its very name as a set of rules which putatively regulate the lives of convicts. It is not a theoretical construct, a set of rules contrived by a sociological theorist for the express purpose of generating the observed behaviour of conducts, but is rather something found *within the social setting* by the researcher. Though the researcher has found the code, it is not a sociologist's discovery, at least not in the sense that nobody knew such a thing was there before some sociologist found it. It is a discovery for sociologists only in the sense that they did not know about such a thing until they started to investigate the low life, prisons etc. Then they found that amongst those involved in these areas of society the code was something already known about. The code was commonplace and familiar fact of life amongst such people, something that they would talk of as such, which they would identify as the code. If a researcher, as Lawrence Wieder did, enters a social setting such as a half-way house for parolees, he will discover, again, that the code looms large in activity there. How will he discover this? Suppose he is to make an empirical investigation, knowing nothing about the setting he is to investigate. He has to find out how this is organized: how does he do so?

In beginning a study the researcher will be rather like the lodger we mentioned above, he will see a great many activities going on but will feel that he does not really understand their proper sense and that those who are native to the setting will have a better sense than he of what is really going on. There will be nothing for it but to watch the activities, listen to the talk and ask questions where he can. In the half-way house setting, the talk would make reference to 'the code' and in this way the researcher would make a first discovery of the existence of the code, discovering it in the talk of the participants, hearing about it from them. Of course, hearing of the code may give a sense that there is a moral order which regulates the life of the convicts but it leaves one in possession of only a title for the code. One knows that it is called, 'the code' but one does not know in what it consists, nor how it governs the life of those allegedly subject to it.

However, the researcher is now oriented in his research via the assumption that there is some patterning principle which presumably guides the lives of those he studies. Grasping the code will enable the researcher to make much more sense of what is going on around him, how the fact of the code affects the lives of both inmates and staff of the institution, but the nature of the code is yet to be identified.

The process of inquiry is one that takes place in time. It is not, however, one which the researcher can organize in appropriately segregated ways. It is not, for example, that the researcher can first identify the pattern of regular behaviour in the community and then when that has been done identify the culture of the community. He is engaged, simultaneously, in identifying both behaviour and culture.

This is not because it is practically inconvenient for him to separate the two activities, but because it is impossible, practically, for him to do so. Remember, the researcher does not grasp what is definitely happening before his eyes *until* he has begun to get some understanding of the code and what it is. Things happen and people talk about them, and in talking about them they make numerous and varied mentions of the code. The researcher feels that there is more going on here than he can appreciate because he has no definite sense of what the code is, and it is only when he can understand what the references to the code are about that he will be able to understand what they really mean, and what has really been going on.

The kind of reasoning involved here is that which Garfinkel calls the documentary method, in which particular events and activities are used to document the presence of an underlying pattern or structure, as the particular occurrences in the half-way house are used to evidence and explicate the existence of a code regulating the life of convicts. In one instance, a member of staff asks an inmate a question, but there is no answer. Appeal to the code allows the silence in response to the question to be construed as a refusal to answer, since to give an answer would perhaps involve being seen as helping staff or informing on fellow cons and both of these are forbidden by the code. So it is appeal to the code which identifies the absence of an answer as a motivated occurrence (rather than as a mishearing, failure to hear of something else.) At the same time, though, the fact that the absence of an answer can be seen as a failure to answer shows that the code is in operation, testifies that cons live by the code, and gives some demonstration of what the code says and requires. It shows, for example, that cooperation with staff and giving information about other inmates are both proscribed.

The researcher does not, then, enter the setting with the capacity to adequately identify and describe the activities which make up its daily life and round. He can of course make *some* description of what is happening but it will not characterize things for what they 'really are' in the setting under study. The researcher has to learn how to correctly, *competently*, describe the setting and he has to learn this from the people who live its life. They have to instruct him in how to talk about them in the same way on his own part. If the researcher described events without reference to the code, then his talk would be treated by participants as naivete, as evidence that he did not understand the realities of life within the scene and was unable to recognize what was really taking place at any time. Being able to describe events in terms of the code enables one to be counted, amongst participants, as one who knows how the local social structure works.

The researcher does not relate to the activities under observation as a complete spectator, for the code is identified through being given instruction in it. Remember, the code recurrently figures in the talk and it is through that talk that parties tell each other how to understand the code and its operation, explain to one another what the code really requires or just how it applies in this or that case. They teach each other how to see the activities of inmates in terms of the convict code and how to see the workings of the convict code in the activities of inmates. The researcher is instructed in the same way through talk with those being studied, can learn for himself the character of the code through partaking as hearer and speaking in the continual process of telling the code which permeates the dealings in which the code features, i.e. the daily round of the half-way house.

Garfinkel's strictures against supposing that a normative order can be specified in so many words should be borne in mind. It is not to be supposed that any participant could recite some exhaustive set of rules-of-the-code and could detail just how these would apply to each and any possible event. Though the existence of the code is, from their point of view, definite enough, what it says and requires cannot be specified in so many words. People can say something about what the code requires and can give an assurance that when things happen they will know if and how the code is relevant but will not be able, in advance, definitely to say all that the code is and requires. Their telling is governed by an et cetera clause, a recognition that the code involves more than they can specifically say and a requirement that people wait and see how things go in order that they will see, with more definiteness and specificity what the code is like. The telling of the code is not something done before and in preparation for entry into the setting, nor is it at any point undertaken in a systematic way. The telling is done during and over the course of the settings daily life and as an integral part of that life. Nor is it done for its own sake, as if the existence of the code were being established as a matter of academic interest. It is done because an awareness of the code and its ways is deemed an indispensable part of competent practical conduct within the setting. The code is, from the point of view of the settings inhabitants, an objective feature of their lives together and one which must be taken into account in organizing actions, in deciding what to do on this or that occasion. The business of telling the code is itself *organized into* the activities of the social setting in which it occurs.

In sum, then, this investigation seeks to say something about what a moral order is. (1) The convict code is described as something which is an oral tradition: it is a way of talking about the activities of a group of people, and it is maintained and perpetuated through being spoken, through being told and, thereby, transmitted to others. (2) The relationship between the code and the setting it regulates is one of mutual elaboration. Activity in and observation of the setting are ways of acquiring a progressively full sense of what the code is and how it works, and a progressive awareness of that also gives an increasing capacity to identify actions for what they are, and to revise one previous conceptions of what one had seen in the direction of what will now count as a more accurate grasp on the nature of events. (3) The code is embedded in the setting, it is to be evidenced and identified in endless and multifarious ways in the things that people do and say. (4) The investigation of the code involves, if we may adopt a coinage of Garfinkel's used to describe the inquiries of astronomers, extracting the animal from the foliage. Just as someone looking to find an animal in a wood has to be able to pick out the animal from the surroundings which may conceal it, so an astronomer looking for a particular kind of stellar object has to pick out from all the details the relevant bits which evidence the presence of that object. Comparably, the researcher seeking to identify the convict code has to be able to pick it out from all the dense, entangled details which make up the daily life of the half-way house.

To restate the premiss of this bit of the argument, ethnomethodology shifts the focus in the contemplation of what are usually called structure and culture. It shifts it away, first, from the assumption that the basic problematical question is whether one is to explain the other to the view that the first problem is a descriptive one: how is one to specify, properly, the properties of both structure and culture? The study of the convict code goes at just those tasks, of saying as specifically as it can what the organization of the daily round is and what the constituents of the moral order are. These are less than easily resolved matters and far from providing residual difficulties they relate to out basic understanding of how social settings work. Secondly, attention moves from arguments about causal and explanatory connections towards organizational ones. The inquiry into the convict code seeks to say how activities and the code that governs them are *organizationally* interrelated, how the code is embedded in the setting and how the setting explicates, i.e. reveals, the existence and nature of the code.

These arguments should enable us to nail one further chronic misunderstanding, which again involves casting ethnomethodology on one side of a dualism that it rejects. Accurately, there are two very closely related dualisms which have provided the stuff of major and long standing sociological controversy. They are those that oppose the individual to society and, macro-sociology to micro-sociology. Ethnomethodology is imagined to focus upon the individual to the neglect of social structure, and the face-to-face encounter at the expense of its organizational environment. However, the example just dealt with should show it cannot cast itself in those terms, for the very notion of the documentary method means that individual action and organizational environment are inseparable, that an action is, from a sociological point of view, *necessarily* action-in-a-social-structure, such that one cannot make sense of what is happening in any local situation without recognition of its relation to a social setting. Thus, for example, one of the things about indexicality is that one does not understand an utterance and then see if it fits in to some language, one understands an utterance by recognizing it for an utterance-in-a-given-language. Thus, the researcher into the half-way house knows *from the outset* of the investigations that these are actions in and of the personnel of an establishiment, the half-way house, and his task is to find in those actions the organization of that setting. Consequently, the problem of individual-versus-society, macrosociology-versus-microsociology is not one that requires philosophical solution but is one that is resolvable in the work of sociological description, which is remorselessly reliant upon the documentary method of reasoning.

We have used the example of the convict code, and this is a report on a field study, and this may give some readers reason to doubt the accuracy of that last claim, that documentary method pervades reasoning about social structures. After all, fieldwork is a qualitative method and such methods are notoriously soft, not to say sloppy: quantitative methods can avoid such difficulties. Garfinkel thinks not, for he thinks the documentary method is requisite to identifying the actual character of the events which make up phenomena in the first place. Whatever kind of methods one might use in the manipulation of one's data one will have to have ways of saying what definitely took place in order to have facts that can be processed by ones methods and to do that one will have to resort to what one already, commonsensically, knows in the application of the documentary method. He tries to show this through the example of coding organizational files. Researchers seek to establish things about what organizations do, what effects they have etc., on the basis of examining records that the organizations keep. The information in the records must be extracted and coded, but it is a feature of files that they involve an assortment of information and a variety of materials and these have to be read as showing or telling what really happened in particular cases and on actual occasions. However, what the files say or tell depends as much on how you read them as on what is in them, since the materials which make them up can be combined in different ways and understood to show/tell different things. There is no rule as to just how documents collected in a file are to be combined, so the fact different connections between them can be made gives rise to different imaginable possibilities as to what might really have happened in an instance. Let us take a simple example: one of the ways in which people can write documents is in such a way that they can be read otherwise than it appears they should be read. Thus in writing an academic reference, for example, it is entirely possible to write one that can be read as if it was entirely approving but which, *for those in the know,* is to be understood as really saying under no circumstances appoint this candidate. For example, 'is a man of deep conviction' might be intended to mean is unbelievably 'awkward and opinionated as a colleague'. Someone reading such a letter, then, might find it wholly equivocal: does it mean what it appears to say or does it contain a coded meaning? In this, and other ways, documents in a file can create numerous imaginable possibilities as to the nature of the events they report and there is no way, from the documents themselves, to determine which are the correct readings. People doing the coding have, then, and *if they are to settle on any single reading which, if they are to code the stuff, they will have to,* will be obliged to invoke their own common sense, appeal to their sense of what people like this will actually say, what they could realistically be expected to do, how in reality rather than imagination they act and so forth. In other words, it will have to be assumed that the organization of the social structure which produced the documents is already known to the inquirer as a condition of being able, satisfactorily, to assign determinate sense to the materials being processed. The operation of documentary method involves, in the case of organizational records, seeing the papers in the file as signs of the pattern of organizational behaviour, but also as acquiring their sense from their place within the organization's structure. The use of the documentary method is something no less essential to quantitative than to qualitative researches.

ACCOUNTABLE ACTIVITIES

The exposition of the instance of the convict code is a most useful way of explaining that other supposed key term of ethnomethodology, namely reflexivity. It also enables us to make a further linkage back to our arguments about the initial assumptions underlying the programme.

We have argued that ethnomethodology undertakes the investigation of the social organization of the world of daily life, as that is encountered in mundane experience. This begins with the recognition that the world of daily life is encountered as an objective environment of everyday activities, and its objectivity is known in terms of common-sense understandings of social settings, through a practical grasp of what things are like and how things are done around here. The fundamental feature of the world of daily life is, then, that it is an environment which makes sense or is intelligible. In saying that it makes sense we are saying no more than that people living in society are able to see what is happening before their very eyes, to assign a determinate character to events they witness—they can, that is, say what is really happening here. This is all argued without presupposing that ethnomethodology must in any way endorse the understandings or conclusions of people in society: it adopts a policy very much akin to phenomenological bracketing: since it is concerned to see how people determine, *to their satisfaction,* how things really are, it can suspend interest in the question of whether they are in any ultimate sense right to be satisfied in that way.

However, in reviewing the shift from Parsons to Schutz, we argued that the assumption that the sense or meaning of activities was given in them had to be suspended also. If it is to be consistent with its assumptions in developing its study policies, then ethnomethodology cannot begin with the assumption that the members of society are determining a sense which is already present in the world of daily life, we must, rather, assume that the are *making* that sense. Instead of asking, then, how people passively make sense of daily life, we ask 'how do people *give* sense to the activities of daily life?' In research terms, this means asking: how do people in society organize their activities in such a way that they make mutual sense, how do people do things in such ways that others can recognize them for what they are? More specifically still, it means that the general investigative question which any sociologist might ask, namely 'how are social actions organized' is replaced by ethnomethodologys query: how do people organize their social actions in such a way that sense can be made of them? This, naturally, makes a considerable difference to the way in which you examine any activity.

This last idea is the one which is contained in the idea of accountability. To talk of social actions as accountable is to talk of them as observable and reportable, to say that they are such that people can see them for what they are and can tell each other about them. This is precisely what the discussion of the convict code was about, the way in which people come to be able to see what is really going on around them and to describe it to each other in ways that will be accepted as plausible and correct. Ethnomethodology says a little more than that actions are accountable, as though this were a feature which they sometimes just happened to possess. It would want to insist upon their *essential* accountability: social organization *has to be* accountable to participants. After all, being able to see what is really going on is an indispensable precondition of action, of being able to orient oneself within a social scene and to carry on its life. Therefore, we cannot study social actions and their accountability as though these were two discrete topics, for they are one-and-the-same: describing how actions organize themselves such that they are observable and reportable is just the way, from ethnomethodology's point of view, of describing how they organize themselves.

The fact that members of a social setting give descriptions of it comes as no news to sociologists. They have long sought to profit from the fact that you can find out about social life by asking people to talk about it (though that has perhaps turned out rather more fraught than they thought). The novelty in the idea of accountability is not in noticing that people tell about their activities, but in proposing that the relationship is reflexive and that the describing of social activities is part and parcel of the activities so described. Again, a shift of interest is involved, away from whether the descriptions people give of what they are doing are true ones and toward the question of how they are, organizationally speaking, related to the activities they describe. It ought to be clear enough that this is the gist of the account of the convict code, that the telling of the code is something entirely intrinsic to the life of the half-way house, and that the investigation inspects the way that the telling of the code fits into the affairs of the house.

The mistake would be to think that this is a recommendation to look at the accounts people give of their actions, rather than at the organization of their activities themselves. This mistake would lead to the suspicion that all we can know about social life is what people tell us, and that we must therefore be wholly dependent on their stories. If such stories were not true then that fact would impact on sociology with a vengeance. However, the recommendation is not to study peoples accounts, but to study *accounting practices*. Rather than relying on what people tell us about their activities, we study the ways in which they organize themselves so that they can tell us about the things they do. It is a way of taking a different slant on whatever activities we examine, ensuring that we will notice features of them which are otherwise neglected. Specifically, it invites us to attend to those aspects of any activity which are involved in arranging it so that people will be able to recognize it for what it is.

Take, for example, one of Garfinkel's most recent studies from amongst the collection of investigations into science. The discussion is of the discovery of a pulsar and the paper describes the activities in the observatory the night the discovery was made. The discovery was subsequently written up. A query which has in recent years very much bothered sociology of science is about the relationship between scientific reports and scientific work. Can one reconstruct the nature of science from a reading of scientific reports? Do they accurately report what really goes on in laboratories, observatories etc.? These questions, naturally, preserve an interest in the correspondence relationship between the description and thing described: do these two correspond, are things as they are described? Garfinkel offers the possibility of something else altogether, a recognition that the laboratory and observatory work is not just arbitrarily connected to the written report, that it does not just happen that the work in the scientific inquiry is a routine generator of written work; the eventual production of a written report is an objective of the investigation. The eventual report of a course of scientific inquiry is indeed a description of that inquiry, but it is also a product of that inquiry, and it is observably the case that the inquiry is organized to produce that report. A piece of scientific research does not go its merry way, complete itself and then get written up, for the work is organized throughout with a concern for the fact that it will have to be written up, and the way in which the work is done will make provision and preparation for the eventual writing up. Records will be kept, notes will be made, writing will be part of the work of the inquiry. It is not, either, that the writing is done by the parties to the inquiries for the sake of making a personal record of their activities on a particular night in the observatory. It is done in orientation to others, as a way of letting other people know and enabling them to see what the researchers have achieved. In that respect, it seeks to tell the events in the observatory in a particular way, to show what, in terms of matters of interest to the astronomical community, the night's work came to, namely the discovery of a particular kind of stellar object. It is a fundamental feature of the organization of scientific inquiries that they are reportable to others in the scientific community.

Scientific work, as an integral and central part of its nature, is a self-reporting activity and it is as such that ethnomethodology contemplates it. Rather than set out to examine scientific work and see if reports on it are true or proposing that since science is self-reporting we can rely on the reports it produces and need not examine its activities for ourselves, it proposes that we examine those activities and reports in a particular way, namely as providing the organization-and-product of a self-reporting system which leads us to look in a fresh way at how activities (such as those making up the daily life of science) hang together.

One standard, and to ethnomethodologists somewhat ironic response to the studies we have been discussing is to try to incorporate them within standard sociological frameworks and topic areas. Wieders study, for example, is often represented as an illustration of the power of the deviant sub-culture, while the studies of science are used to show the social construction of reality. The irony in this attempt to fit ethnomethodological

studies into conventional sociology is that it completely misses the motivation which underlies the work and which gives it its rationale and its
distinctiveness. The motivation is what we earlier called Garfinkel's determination to follow the animal in sociological investigations. The study
policies which we summarized at the end of the previous chapter were
designed to allow investigators to pick up its trail, so to speak. However,
once on the animal's track, how are we to get close eneough to examine it in
detail? How can we approach near enough without frightening it back into
the foliage? That is the problem, and therein lies the difficulty of any
ethnomethodological study. The signal achievement of Conversation
Analysis is that it managed to solve this problem for its phenomena.
Through its methods of analysis, a beginning was made on the sociological
description of the specifics and particularities of conversation as it is
ordinarly found. It is to these beginnings that we now turn.

5

Conversation's organization

INVESTIGATING CONVERSATIONAL MATERIALS

Though it will need some linking to show how the work done in conversational analysis connects with the arguments that have gone before, there is a natural continuity between the topics we have just been discussing and those we shall shortly take up. In this chapter, though, the somewhat paradoxical character of our strategy will be most apparent, for conversational analysis prides itself more than anything upon sticking to the detailed specifics of instances of talk and holding back from involvement in generalized discussion — but we shall say hardly anything about these specifics. However, it is in dealing with conversational analysis that we think the value of our strategy will also be most apparent. We have been more concerned to get at the motivation guiding the steps ethnometholodology takes, in the hope that recognition of this will enable readers to see more sense, design and cogency in particular studies than they would otherwise do. Exposition of the detail of studies has then been sacrificed in pursuit of clarification of ideas. In the case of conversational analysis we think it altogether pointless to try to impress people with its achievements by showing them its specific inquiries since it is in seeing any virtue whatever in such studies that most sociological readers have the greatest difficulty.

We will, of course, give some outline of the things conversational analysts have done, but we have gone for giving a flavour of the thinking that lies behind these studies in the hope that this will persuade people to look more sympathetically and comprehendingly at the studies that result and, perhaps, give them a much clearer idea of the scale on which conversational analysis achievements stack up as quite considerable ones. For many ethnomethodologists they amount to the most substantial accomplishments of inquiry so far. They are not altogether uncontroversial, and these is certainly room for argument as to how far conversational analysis now owes any allegiance whatever to ethnomethodology's programme. It may have in important part originated in that, but it has developed as a mature and autonomous pursuit in its own right and need not therefore consider itself bound by ethnomethodology's requirements. Indeed, its own commitment to faithfulness to its own phenomenon, commonplace conversation, is what guides its methodological and analytical decisions, not the requirements of a programme. Properly viewed, ethnomethodology's programme is a way into studies, not a set of specifications about how they should be done, and hence not a set of binding requirements which override whatever measures the studies themselves make necessary.

However, amongst many ethnomethodologists conversational analysis stands in highest regard. The work of the late Harvey Sacks, though still largely unpublished more than a decade after his death, is looked upon with something approaching awe and the close collaboration between Sacks and two colleagues, Emmanuel Schegloff and Gail Jefferson, in the analysis of conversational turn taking is ranked as ethnomethodology's most finished and accomplished achievement to date.

In sociology more generally, by contrast, conversational analysis does not meet with anything like the same esteem. Sacks's work is not at all well known, especially that mass of transcribed lectures made between 1964 and 1972 which is indispensable to a recognition of the scope and character of Sacks's thought. Conversational analysis has achieved noteriety rather than respect, and many regard it as derisory and perverse. It looks, from the outside, like something trivial and trite and dead easy to do.

If some were to read through Sacks's lectures they would find that an awfully large proportion of them is spent on examining a transcript of a couple of hours of conversation between some adolescents — pseudonymously identified as Ken, Roger, Jim, Al and Louise — in therapy with an adult, Dan. At one stage the better part of a semester was given over to examining a story — The baby cried. The mummy picked it up — told by a small child. The kind of transcript examined by Sacks looks like this (though this is not one of the transcripts Sacks worked on)†:

1	Jenny:	⎡Saltbehrn.˙hhh
2	Vera:	⎣uhOhh:::::::: 'eed⎡f'gott'n⎤
3	Jenny:	⎣En I lef⎣t a neo:te.

4   Jenny: No I left a ↓ neote f'Mahthew saying em ˙hhh eh– I le-
            eh (·)

5   B'cuz ah know ees a lit'l divil yihkno:w, ˙hh so I
            bahhh! I

6   (had left a neote t'sa:y thet (·) I'd be ↑ ba:ck. soo:n,
            ˙hh

7   En I put the ti:me onnit. I said I've jus taken Ivan
            t'the:

8   (0.3) centuh.

9   (·)

10   Vera: Yes.

11   Jenny: Th'spohrt centuh.

12   Vera: °Ahhh:::::.°

13   (·)

14   Jenny: An',

15   (0.7)

16   Jenny: Well u (·) °What ti:me was it,°˙h Ah leftche et about
            twenty

17   tih fi:ve.

18   (0.4)

19   Vera: Ah dunno what time it was J⎡enny ah cahn't remem-⎤
            ⎣buh really,   ⎦

20   Jenny: ⎣°Ye:s,° I left here et twenty⎦

21   t'five en there wz nob'ddy i:n.Now ah tha'wee w'd'a
            kem with

22   me y'se⎡e, ˙hhh=

23   Vera: ⎣Ye:s,

24   Vera: =Y⎡es,

25   Jenny: ⎣En ah'v En ah picked Ivan up et te:n to:,

26   (1.0)

As can be seen, the talk has been transcribed (in this case by Gail Jefferson) with the most meticulous care, even its most detailed and slight features being picked up. Even if most sociologists were prepared to start examining the things these people say (and most of them are not) then they certainly would not want to spend their time inspecting the pauses, false starts and other things that seem quite irrelevant to the sense of what is

† See the Appendix at the end of this chapter for an example of the transcript conventions used in Conversational Analysis.

being said. They simply cannot see the point of looking so closely at such materials. They cannot, either, see the point in making assorted remarks in an haphazard way about boring, commonplace, tedious, inconsequential talk, especially when those who do seem bent on disregarding entirely the few things that seem of real sociological interest. What results from the work on conversation does not seem much more interesting or appealing than the materials or the process of inspecting them closely. The most substantial result of these inquiries has been a set of rules for taking turns in conversation, which are specified as follows:

(1) For any turn, at the initial transition-relvance place of an initial turn-constructional unit:

(a)   If the turn-so-far is so constructed as to involve the use of a, current speaker selects next, technique, then the party so selected has rights, and is obliged, to take next turn to speak, and no others have such rights or obligations, and transfer occurs at that place;

(b)   If the turn-so-far is so constructed as not to involve the use of a, current speaker selects next, technique, self-selection for next speakership may, but need not, be instituted; with first starter acquires rights to a turn, and transfer occurs at that place;

(c)   If the turn-so-far is so constructed as not in involve the use of a, current speaker selects next, technique, then current speaker may, but need not continue, unless another self-selects.

(2) If, at the initial transition-relevance place of an initial turn constructional unit, neither 1(a) nor 1(b) has operated, and, following the provision of 1(c), current speaker has continued, then the rule-set [a–c] reapplies at next transition-relevance place, and recursively at each next transition-relevance place, until transfer is effect. (H. Sachs, E. Schegloff and G. Jefferson, 'A Simplest Systematics for the Organisation of Turn Taking in Conservation' *Language*, 1974, p. 704).

They say, in less technical vein, that if someone who is speaking has possibly finished saying what they want to say, then someone else can start to speak and that if someone has been specifically selected by the current speaker (by being named, for example) then they can and should speak next. Failing that, anyone may attempt to get the floor for themselves by starting to talk. Should that not happen, then the current speaker may continue. These rules are to be applied, and in that order, at *every* point at which a speaker may possibly have finished a turn.

These rules, in our experience, often receive a so what? reaction. They seem the sort of thing that anybody knows and that, therefore, almost anybody could have written down for themselves. There seems no great achievement in specifying rules such as these. However, once again these reactions perhaps originate in the failure to rcognize that a change in objectives and problematic must necessarily effect a change in conceptions of what an achievement is. At least against the background of ethnomethology's programme that the merit of and difficulty in articulating such rules can be appreciated. The outcome, the focusing of attention most closely on turn taking arrangements in ordinary conversations derives from the commitment to making studies, to putting the examination of the phenomenon first, which we describe in the previous chapter. The implementation of ethnomethodology's programme requires the direct inspection of commonplace activities, and Sacks's work and conversational analysis devote themselves to the investigation of that most commonplace of activities, ordinary conversation. It is often called natural conversation just to emphasize that the materials investigated have not been contrived for any sociological purposes but are taken, so to speak, as they come.

The best way to achieve a direct inspection of ordinary talk is to tape-record it, and then one can examine it pretty closely, repeatedly and in some detail. Furthermore, the difficulty involved in specifying something like a rule system for the organization of turn taking is hard to estimate if one has not tried to do that or something similar. It is common for people being introduced to computer programming to be given the assignment of writing out instructions for a simple and commonplace task such as changing a car tyre in order that they may gain a sense not of how complicated changing a car tyre is, but of what a difficult and complicated task it is to write a set of instructions for something as simple as that. Getting out a set of rules for something as basic as turn taking is by no means as easy as the end product makes it look. In taking up such materials, which are selected by virtue of being those to hand at the time, Sacks and his colleagues were not undertaking to make them objects of standard sociological interest. They did not intend, that is, to begin from assumptions about the bearing that the study of ordinary talk might have on the established problems of sociology. Could one see anything of interest to the sociologist in such uneventful chit-chat? Asking that question presupposed that the kind of interest sociologists could take in a phenomenon was already well defined, *even before they had inspected the phenomenon*. Consequently, before anything much was known about a phenomenon decisions were being made as to what would comprise a proper sociological treatment of it. To Harvey Sacks, this seemed to have gotten just about everything the wrong way round. The way to investigate a phenomenon was not to begin from conclusions about what the study of it would have to yield, but to begin by examining the phenomena itself to see what kind of character it has and what conclusions it could actually support. Of course, there is some point in electing to begin by attending to ordinary talk in that Garfinkel's programme offered the possibility of looking at ordinary language in its own right, of seeing how parties to it made sense of each others utterances. In addition, sociological analysis though it introduced some jargon of its own takes place largely through the use of categories of our common and ordinary language but attention has not been given to how these categories are used in everyday speech. Conversation need not have been the place to go next in developing Garfinkel's ideas, but there were some things which made it somewhat more directly connected to them than other possibilities.

The thing which baffles critics is: what is the interest in the materials of conversational analysis, who can be interested in such empty talk? The *intrinsic* interest of conversational materials is not necessarily any greater to those who analyse them than to those who refuse to do so. Conversational analysis did not get going because of an expectation that the materials being studied would prove to be much more interesting than they first seemed, that one would find that what was going on in the talk was really much more significant and profound than it might seem. Sociologists of other persuasions have tried to find interest in such materials by, for example, seeing conversational exchanges as (perhaps covert) struggles for power and control, thus linking ordinary talk to such recognized sociological themes as domination and control. Conversational analysts have resolutely resisted any attempt to endow the conversations they study with this kind of seeming importance. If the talk they examine is empty and tedious, they can acknowledge this, because the interest of the materials for sociological analysis does not derive from their intrinsic significance but from the fact that they represent instances of real-worldly occurrences which are possible within the organization of talk and which must therefore be encompassed by *any* account which seeks to provide for how, generally, ordinary talk may be. Indeed, if the talk does prove trivial and vapid, then this might be an advantage fro the point of view of the problems to be tackled. Indeed, what the talk is about is, for most purposes, quite irrelevant. The focal concern is with the analysis of the organization of a commonplace activity.

Three futher links with ethnomethodology are important to seeing some point to conversational analysis.

The first is the emphasis on the gap between research and phenomenon. As we argued, sociological investigations often fail to work out, as methods find it very difficult to locate the organizational properties of their phenomenon. It might be argued that this is so because sociology is a nascent discipline and because its problems are large and complex and one cannot therefore expect it to be able to get a tight grip on the things it tries to study. On the other hand, it can be suggested that not all the problems sociology faces need to be large and complex, that some simple and basic ones can be identified and worked at and one might hope, in those, to make the researches work out in a much more rigorous way.

Further, if the big problems of sociology are to be solved it may be that the way to them is to be found by starting a good way off, with problems on a much smaller scale which can be tackled and carried through to solution. Ordinary talk, as that occurs in commonplace scenes, is something on which data can easily be collected. A short recording of some minutes of talk will give more than enough materials to allow prolonged close consideration. Hence, there is no need to spend immense amounts of time collecting unwieldy bodies of materials which may well prove, after they have been assembled, less than suitable for answering the questions that are to be put to them. The ready collection of conversational materials, just involving the recording of whatever people happen to be saying, means that one is not bound to put certain questions to the data (as one is in collecting materials for many other kinds of sociological inquiry.) One can examine the data to see what kinds of questions it is suitable to answer, and hence can articulate examinations of it in such a way that they will invariably be responsive to and answerable by the data available. The project is, then, to identify the organization of commonplace conversation. The point, to conceive a project for sociological inquiry which can be carried out in detail.

In at least one way the project is unprecedented: nowhere else in sociology has anyone sought to put together a thoroughly systematic investigation into the organization of a particular phenomenon. Hence, Sacks's project was both ambitious and modest. It was modest in that it set itself tasks which might be considered elementary for a serious empirically oriented discipline, but ambitious in that it sought to achieve something which, in terms of the integrity of investigating and analysing its phenomena, had not elsewhere been matched in sociology.

The second important connection with ethnomethodology was in attention to conversation as a practical activity.

Ethnomethodology studies the world of daily life. It identifies the world known to common sense as the visible and visibly objective environment of daily life. Common sense identifies, for members of a community, the facts of life, i.e. those circumstances which are the immutable and unavoidable conditions of life. The members of society act within the world of daily life, and their action there is practical. They have things to do, and they have to carry out whatever projects they have in an environment which is given to them, which is not of their own choosing (however palatable or otherwise it might be to them). If they are to be able to act, then they have to be able to manage the circumstances provided by the social setting, to be able to put their activities together under whatever conditions are given by the continuing operations of the social setting they inhabit.

The distinction has been made between the natural attitude and the theoretical attitude. The former is the attitude people in society take toward their environment, the latter is that which the theorist can take and which allows exemption from many of the requirements of the natural attitude. The theorist can we have noted, have a God-like control of his theoretical world, can stipulate what will count in it, what considerations can have relevance, and the terms in which things are to be connected. The theorist constructs a simplified world, from which many things must and will be excluded. The practical actor under the natural attitude does not have this kind of power and cannot specify what the circumstances under which action will have to take place, cannot dictate what will be relevant to what, nor how one thing will affect another. The practical actor has to do *whatever* is required under *whatever* circumstances are given/found if things are to get done.

Since ethnomethodology has given up the goal of constructing a theoretically simplified world that will explain social behaviour and is concerned with describing the organization of daily life and action performed under the auspices of the natural attitude it has no interest in seeking to specify how, under theoretically simplified conditions, actions might be carried out or interrelated. It must attend, instead, to the description of how, under what are for the perpetrator *real worldly conditions* courses of action are organized and carried out. It is not satisfactory for ethnomethodology — as it might be for some other sociology — to say how in principle some action might be done or some outcome of action made possible. Ethnomethodology, if it is to follow out its own programme, must be able to say how *in actuality* a course of conduct might be realized or a certain outcome assured. The relevance of conditions to understanding practical action is not to be decided on the basis of their interest or otherwise to the considerations entertained by a sociological theory, it is to be decided by their indispensability or otherwise to the accomplishment of the actions involved. Ethnomethodology seeks to see *exactly what* someone has to do to carry out an action, *exactly what* has to be done to produce and reproduce the regularities of social life.

A third connection with ethnomethodology is through the notion of self-organizing settings. Though this expression was not given the prominence that caused indexical and reflexive to stand out as apparent key words it does formulate an idea which is much more important than they in understanding why many studies take the shape they do and especially why conversational analysis takes the line it does.

To talk of a self-organizing setting is to give research priority to examining the ways in which a social setting *composes itself*, asking just what specifiable course of action make up the setting and how their interrelations build up into and sustain whatever might be identified as the organized structures of the setting. Instead of asking the more usual question, why does the setting possess this feature? with the intent of determining what purpose or function it might serve, we ask how does the setting make it happen that this is a stable feature of its organization? with the intent of seeing how activities form and maintain a pattern. Thus, a good example of the description of a setting as self-organizing is Melvin Pollners description of pleading in traffic court. If we studied the succession of pleadings in trafficce court, we might find that there was a pattern to these, that pleas were characteristically done in much the same way. If we look to find out how this pattern of pleading is produced we can see (a) that those waiting to have their case tried can witness previous pleas and can see how the pleading was done and (b) that those previous pleadings can be treated as precedents, showing how pleading is properly to be done, the judge playing an active role in instructing defendants in how they are to make their plea. Thus, the ecology of the setting makes visible the activities of judge and defendant to those waiting their turn and enables the flow of cases to follow a standard form (or something like it). Indeed, the courtroom is more than self-organizing, it is self-explicating, for its organizational arrangements make explicit to people how they are supposed to behave within it.

Conversational analysis is, if we may put it this way, more concerned with utterances than with speakers and hearers. It is much less concerned with talk as a relation between persons than it is with conversation as a relation betwen utterances. It is, in line with what we have just been saying about self-organizing settings, devoted to examining the ways in which utterances can relate to one another, with the ways in which utterances can make up interwoven patterns and with the ways in which utterances, in their interrelation, build up those patterns. Hence, if one finds that conversations are units, that they have a beginning, middle and end, and that this is a standard, reproduced feature of conversation, then the object is to see how any single conversation can provide itself with that organizationn, how its utterances can make up such a unified form, and how those utterances produce, once again, the standard form of a conversation's course: just what things are said to begin a conversation, just how do those things involve movement from the beginning to the middle of a conversation, and once a conversation is in full flow, what kinds of sayings will bring it to an orderly conclusion? Such answers require us to examine the various kinds of utterances that there are, and the organizational implications that their properties have. Thus, in Schegloff's account of the opening of telephone conversation of which we give a few further details below, he was examining the openings of conversational sequences through the study of the answering of telephone calls. He came to analyse the answering of the telephone in terms of an utterance pair, summons and answers. Such utterances go together in the sense that summons requires an answer, a summons is done (so to speak) in search of an answer.

The neat thing about this pair, from the point of view of initiating an exchange of talk, is that if a summons is answered, then the summoner is required to speak again: thus, a summons–answer pair has the organizational potential to generate further talk. It is in this sense that conversational analysis is more concerned with utterances than speakers, being concerned with the ways in which utterances can combine themselves into unified, internally organized, developing exchanges. In order to see what organizational possibilities of arrangement are involved in utterances there is often little need to pay attention to the character or motivation of the speakers, for the questions about the interrelation of utterances are independent of those about the interests, purposes, aims etc. of speakers. Of course, these are not entirely excluded, but when they enter into the discussion they do so in a subordinate respect, in order to allow determination of the character of an utterance or in order to show how a particular kind of utterance can exhibit a particular thought, intention etc. Thus, for example, conversational analysts look at silence, but not in order to discover what motives people have for silence. They are inclined to note, rather, the way in which silence can have rich inferential potential, the way in which a silence, *in relation to the turn taking arrangements of conversation, and the type of utterance which antedates it*, can be used to make inferences of the state of mind of the silent person, for example that they are thinking of an answer, that they are taken aback, that they were not paying attention and so forth.

Again perhaps, these remarks may serve to eliminate some of the puzzlement that conversational analysis creates. The way which most sociologists will find it natural to look at talk is as data providing a means of access to other phenomena: looking at how people talk serves as a way of finding out about various aspects of social structures, hence it is of primary importance to notice who is doing the talking, what circumstances they might be doing it under, what they are doing it for and so forth. However, for conversational analysis, it is *the talk itself* that is the object of attention, to be examined from the point of view of identifying the social organization of talk *as talk*. That problem does not require the same kind of attention to who is doing the talking, why they are doing it etc. Indeed, the question goes the other way around: how can we find out, from talk, what people are doing, why they are doing it, what the salient circumstances are, and so on?

Inquiry into conversation was directed, then, by a desire to see how a real world course of coordinated conduct could be practically organized and how it could build up its own organization. The central problem is, then, one that we will describe as a production problem: how does conversation make itself happen, and how does it provide itself with those features that it exhibits? This was to be done through the close inspection of tape recordings of natural conversations, such that any proposed analysis would have to be strongly compatible with *at least* the evidence provided by whatever materials were to hand. Just how strong a constraint that can be was indicated in Schegloff's paper on sequencing in conversational openings. The materials were a set of recordings of telephone calls, and Schegloff's task was simply that of finding orderliness in their first five seconds. Was there any regularity to the way telephone calls began? It seemed that there was, that a rule like 'answerer speaks first' would do for telephone openings. Except that in a corpus of 500 openings, there was one which did not begin that way. In consequence, Schegloff had to give up his initial rule and develop a new analysis for the whole corpus, one which would not attempt to explain away the irregularity but which would account for it on-a-par with the other occurrences. Anyone who thinks that conversational analysis is just a matter of making random remarks about transcripts and, as such, is pretty easy to do should think again. Anyone who has tried to do it can tell them just how tough it is to get anywhere with.

ANALYSING CONVERSATIONAL SEQUENCE

The first question for conversational analysis must, then, be: do ordinary conversations, as they routinely occur, show any orderliness? The almost immediate answer is, of course, that they do. Take any conversation and one will find that it has order and organization, that it makes sense and has some kind of coherence — enought to mark it out as a unified conversation. Conversational analysts are looking, in the first instance, to see what kind of orderliness a conversation *ordinarily* possesses. They are not seeking for insights which involve noticing features or regularities of conversation which no one has ever noticed before. In the first instance they are overwhelmingly concerned just to notice what anyone would notice, to see the glaring and obvious things. If they are going to examine conversation as something conversationalists do, then it is going to be indispensable to identify the things to which conversationalists are sensitive and to which they attend as a matter course.

And the thing which is most grossly observable about any conversation, something which is almost automatically reflected in the way people transcribe it, is its *sequential* chartacter: a conversation is a progression of utterances, one after other in time. Further, it is instantly notable that the progression of a conversation is a coordinated exercise, that different people contribute different sayings to its course, but that these different sayings are (somehow) related to one another. People thus take turns at talking, and they manage (somehow) to alternate their talkings such that they are not, except briefly, all talking at once, and they manage to alternate the talking in such ways that there is often and for quite long sequences of talk, interconnection between the things said. Finally, at least for our purposes, it is notable that conversations are units, that a particular conversation's progression is from something that is *recognizably* the beginning of a conversation, through utterances which are *recognizably* in the middle of a conversation to what is recognizably that conversation's closing. Hence, a whole conversation has a form (an overall structural organization in the jargon) involving movement from beginning through to closings, but, of course, when any real conversation begins, though the parties may have some notion of things they want to talk about in its course, those who coordinatedly produce the organized unit will have no definite idea of its future course, of what *exactly* and *specifically* they will have to say to each other carry it through its course. The conversation is worked up on the spot, is devised even as it is carried out: it is an improvised activity.

The sheer obviousness of some features of conversation makes them most important to understand. The fact that speakers take turns at talking is obviously something that is essential to any account of how conversation is organized. When Sacks proposes that, in conversation at least, not more than one person speaks at a time, he is sometimes regarded as if he thought he had discovered an hitherto unknown fact about conversation. No such supposition is involved. Sacks himself would be the first to point out that it is not strictly true, in conversation, one party talks at a time (often no one speaks, at other times, several people speak) but insofar as it is true that people take turns at conversation, Sacks is not offering this up as something he has (astoundingly) revealed, but precisely what it is, an obvious and central fact about conversation and, therefore, as something which must play a cenral and consequential role in organizing conversation. That conversation has a turn-by-turn arrangement does not comprise a discovery for conversational analysis, but provides its problem: the specification of conversation's organization as a turn-taking system.

Again the distinctiveness of Sacks's task is worth stressing. Turn-taking arrangements are involved in many activities, but nowhere in the sociological literature will one find a description of just how a specific turn taking arrangement operates, but it is just that which conversational analysis will, if successful, issue in. Further, as far as turn-taking systems go, conversation is one in which turns are circulated, but not according to any prescribed formula, and the turn-taking system which is described will, therefore, have to be one which enables turns to be taken in an orderly but unpredictable way. Hence, the turn-taking system will be one which will distribute turns continuously throughout the conversation: it does not, that is, work by initially distributing an order of turns such that these are then circulated in a fixed pattern.

Conversational analysis's specific inquiries can be classed as being of broadly two kinds. There are those which are concerned with the distribution of turns in conversation, and which are concerned with how conversation operates as a turn-by-turn organization. That is concerned with the local problem of turn distribution: given that someone is now speaking, how is it decided who will speak next, how will this particular utterance relate to the ones that follow it? The second kind of inquiries, to which we have already alluded, are those which have to do with how a whole conversation structures itself as a unit — we called them problems of overall structural organization.

The former kind of problems are those that are dealt with in such an impressively condensed way in the 'Simplest systematic' for turn taking: we quoted the rules which comprise this simplest systematics above. Given that conversation is an activity which almost anyone, including quite small children, drunks and retards, can do, then the practices which govern it must be very simple, ones which can be easily mastered and applied by anyone. Similarly, given that conversation is something that can take place between people of all kinds, then the rules which regulate turn taking must be independent of the social composition of the conversation: consequently, the simple set cited above is just what is sought. These rules enable people to know when it is legitimate for them to start talking, when they can legitimately suppose that a previous speaker has finished and that they can commence their turn. It gives them, too, ways of deciding who speaks next, which of possible candidates for taking a turn should do so, and so on. It also shows why the turn-taking in conversation is not perfectly smooth: there are plenty of occasions on which, in conversation, either no one speaks (there is a pause) or more than one person speaks (there is simultaneous talking) but these occurences tend to be brief. The turn-taking systematics shows that both the frequency and brevity of these occurences are produced and resolved by the application of the rules of turn-taking. Thus, for example, the rules allow someone to start to speak at a point at which a current speaker has possibly finished, but of course a point at which someone may have finished is not necessarily one at which they have finished, and so one speaker may be continuing to talk when another starts up.

Just to ensure that there is no misunderstanding to the effect that the strategy of conversational analysis results in a straightforward rule following account of conversation, it should be pointed out that the specification of the rules for turn-taking is only part of the story. There is, first of all, much argument to show that these are rules which are attended to by the participants in conversation, and there is also — even within the paper formulating the simplest systematics themselves — an insistence that conversation is to be understood in the way that conversationalists themselves orient to, implement and enforce those rules. Conversation is a participant-managed system, and the fact that the parties to it collaboratively generate its organization is the rock-bottom fact.

The strength of the turn-taking strategy is one which we cannot really begin to document here, for its strength is that it allows close and thorough examination of the extensive and detailed organization of conversation. We cannot begin to show just how condensed the statement in the 'Simplest systematic' paper is nor to outline the extent of work on conversational organisation involving it but not even alluded to in that paper. This book is a brief resumé, and its very nature precludes the kind of expansive, careful and detailed exposition needed to bring out the extent, power and subtlety of Sacks's thinking. All that we can do is to advise against reading the 'Simplest systematic' paper as though it embodied, in a simple and easily recoverable sense, what conversational analysis amounts to. In order to be anything like properly understood it needs to be grasped through application, to be approached through an attempt to actually analyse conversational materials to its standards.

As far as the business of overall structural organization — including as it does beginnings — is concerned, then it should be apparent that the work of Schegloff cited above falls within this domain. Of course, it should be apparent that the two kinds of work — those are turn by turn organisation and an overall structure — are thoroughly interconnected for, of course, it is the case that the problem of how the unity of a conversational sequence is constructed cannot be dissociated from the way in which it puts itself together utterance by utterance. The discussion of how the alternation of speakers may be managed, given that one of them has the floor, need not raise the question of how come that speaker is taking a turn, but a consideration of how a conversation is organized as a whole address the question of how someone gets to speak first. Thus, Schegloff's paper is concerned with how a conversation makes a beginning, how people achieve what he calls coordinated entry into converation, through an inspection of two immediately related utterances, the first (summons) and the next (the answer.)

How a conversation will develop, we have said, is not something that is worked out in advance, and the conversations structure is worked up over the course of the talk that comprises it, and so when parties make a start on a conversation they have yet to discover what the course of their talk will be. The way in which they begin their conversation will be important in shaping its subsequent course, though how they begin does not dictate, in some fixed and final sense, how things must go. For example, it is a routine enough feature of conversation that, very early on, the question 'how are you?' is asked, and it is such a routine feature that it is met with the response 'Fine' that many people consider this exchange a ritual. It is also often a ritual in the sense that people ask 'how are you?' out of politeness and expect a bland, neutral answer: they do not want to be told how the other is, especially if that other has bad news. If one asks 'How are you?' and is given some other-than-neutral response such as 'Awful' or 'Great' then one is most likely going to feel obliged to ask 'Why, what happened?' or something equivalent, and then one is going to be involved in hearing about, and talking to, the other's good fortune or misery, whichever it is. The asking of 'How are you' is a decisive moment for conversation, then, in that if an other-than-neutral response is given, then that is going to direct at least a long sequence of talk, if not the whole conversation, to talking about a particular subject matter. If, on the other hand, the ritual, neutral answer is given, then the exchange of 'How are you?' queries stands as a formal step and the conversation can progress to other matters.

The business of making beginnings is a complex and variable one. The placement of things at the beginning of conversations can have significance and can, as we have just indicated, have consequences for the talk's further course. Thus, for example, in telephone calls (which we confine ourselves to for brevity's sake) it is a matter of high priority to establish the identity of the parties to the call and their reasons for making it. Amongst friends, for example, it is an issue as to whether the call is for a reason, or for no particular reason. That the call may be for something specific, and indeed important, like the delivery of some news, is something that is to be established at the outset, as soon as possible, such that something very important can lead to even the expectable exchange of greetings being bypassed with (say) 'You'll never believe what just happened.' If a caller has a reason for a call then this should be indicated at the outset. Those who ring with a reason for the call do not, however, always want that fact to be recognized — they are ringing to ask for something, say — and they often want a call that is for a reason to look like a call for no reason, introducing the reason at some later point as though it were an afterthought to the making of the call. One can see, then, manoeuvring going on around what a call shall be about, and even about who actually made the call. Thus, it is possible for someone who has been called to pre-empt the status of caller by, for example, saying, 'My God, I've been trying to get through to you for the last hour', or 'I've been meaning to call you all week': they put themselves forward as virtual callers. Thus, parties establish what the first thing a telephone call is going to talk about, what — if any — its first topic is going to be, and one could then proceed, if following through the sequential development of conversations progression, to talk about the way topics are selected, initiated, elaborated, closed down, transformed and so forth — as, of course, conversational analysts have done.

A word of warning about the very brief sketch we have given of the way in which the problem of conversational openings has been tackled. We have used psychological sounding words like manouvre and it is, given the way in which readers often jump to quite unjustified conclusions, as if we are employing some kind of competitive, manipulative kind of psychology in which people try to get the edge on each other. Without wanting to deny that this kind of thing may sometimes happen we want to stress that terms like manoeuvre, when used in conversational analysis, have no psychological implications: they are employed as structural notions. If say, someone asks another, 'What's new?', then it is possible to respond to that with 'Nothing, what's new with you?', and it is just a feature of that first question that its asker gives the opportunity to the other to introduce some news or topic worth talking about, and it is equally just a feature of the response that it passes back that opportunity, that (*so to speak*) the second speaker declines the opportunity. Quite long sequences of utterances in which the speakers offer to each other possible ways of introducing a first something to talk about may develop and it is in that respect that we talk about manoeuving without implying that there is, on the conversationalists part, any deliberate effort to avoid being the first person to introduce any topic at all or some particular topic or other.

These sketchy comments on the kind of work done on the overall structural organization of conversation do no more justice to their topic than do our abbreviated comments on the turn-taking system. Our over-riding objective in this section has not been to report on what conversational analysis has done in the way of working out how ordinary conversation organizes itself but to give some idea of the thinking that is behind the work of conversation, thus perhaps making it more intelligible as to why people would want to examine conversation in the close way that these do and of what they hope to achieve by it. After all, there is no point in reciting the accomplishments of conversational analysis to people who have no real understanding of what standards are relevant to the assessment of those accomplishments. We hope that we have given some indication of the standards which conversational analysis sets for itself.

Though we have talked about the elementary and modest character of the inquiries into conversation and acknowledged the possible trivialiy of the content of the materials it deals with, we do not want to sell it short and would certainly reject any suggestion that conversational analysis is therefore less important or interesting than other forms of sociological inquiries which have larger immediate ambitions, take on much larger problems or tackle issues which apparently have more intrinsic significance. If comparisons are to be made here, then the scale of ambitions and the scope of topics surely should not provide the sole criteria. The relationship between ambition and achievement ought to count, as should the adequacy of the treatment to the scope of the topic. It is of little use having very large ambitions and taking on big topics if one is ill-equipped and poorly prepared and if, in the end, one is going to fall far short of the targets one has set oneself. In this respect, conversational analysis has gone for bringing ambition and achievement into line, undertaking a programme of inquiries it can realistically hope to carry through. This is not, however, to be mistaken for a giving up on the grander-seeming aims and subjects, but as a strategy for getting at them altogether more effectively. If they are to be dealt with, then they will have to be worked up to. The point of taking elementary, relatively simple and uncomplicated problems is not to confine us permanently to the consideration of these but to give much more power and cogency to the treatment of advanced, complex and complicated matters. Working on basic and simple problems is a good place to start learning how to come to terms with the advanced and difficult ones.

Important though the availability of natural language might be to the presupposition and work of sociology, especially when these matters are viewed through ethnomethodology's eyes, it is not because of its subject matter that conversational analysis might then command some rather more respectful attention from the sociological community, but by virtue of the kind of methodological problems that it deals with. Those problems, of getting access to and a close acquaintance with the organization of a specific social phenomena are the sorts of problems which a would-be empirical sociology may well have to face on a broad front. If our arguments about the gap between the methods and the phenomena are correct, and it there is indeed a desire and need to have theorizing about social phenomena closely related to the observable properties of social scenes, then the kind of investigation exemplified in conversational analysis will inevitably have to be undertaken sooner or later.

APPENDIX: GUIDE TO THE TRANSCRIPT CONVENTIONS
(contributed by Gail Jefferson)

I. Sequencing

[

A: A:nd the:n, Mister Nevins,
·hh may put his defen⌈se.
P: ⌊Mm,

A single bracket indicates the point at which one utterance is overlapped by another.

[[[

A: ⌈⌈M-hm,
P: ⌊⌊·hhhhh The woman that made the dress I can't say to her . . .

Double brackets indicate that two utterances start simultaneously.

]

P: Well the ⌈thing i:s,────────⌉
A: ⌊that you would l⌐ike

A single right-hand bracket indicates the point at which overlapping utterances or utterance components end *vis-à-vis* one another

=

A: And you walked out of the shop wearing the sandles.=
P: =Yes I did. Yes.

A: I will the:n⌐ask you if there=⌊
P: ⌊Mn
A: =are any questions,

The equal signs indicate no interval between the end of one piece of talk and the start of a next. This convention is used as between one speaker's talk and another's and as between parts of a same speaker's talk.

(0.0)

P: and the date that I actually received them::–::.
(0.7)
A: And you walked out of the shop wearing the sandals.

Numbers in parentheses indicate elapsed time in tenths of seconds.

(·)

A: A:n:d, (·) you're entitled to call any witnesses . . .

The dot in parentheses indicates a very brief silence, say, 1/10 second or less.

II. Sound production

?,.?
,

D: and did you get an extension.

A: you're entitled to call any witness to support your clai::m? if you have any,
,

P: We:ll. (·) I don't know? I suppose...

A: A:n:d, (·) you're entitled to call any witnesses to support your cla::m? if you have any,
,

Punctuation symbols are not used as grammatical markers, but for intonation. So, for example, a 'question' may be transcribed with a comma or a period while question-marks may be used for utterances which are not 'questionss'. The [?] indicates not fully rising intonation

Colons indicate that the prior sound is prolonged. The more colons, the longer the sound.

::	A:	A:n:d, (·) you're entitled to call any witnesses to support your clai::m? if you have any,	*Underscoring* indicates various forms of stressing and may involve pitch and/or volume.
−::	A:	your clai::m	*The relationship between underscore and colons* indicates pitch change (or non-change) in the course of a word. In 'clai::m' pitch rises at the end, in 'clai::m' pitch falls at the end, in 'clai::m' and 'clai::m' pitch does not change in the course of the word, the former being lightly stressed, the latter being heavily stressed.
	H:	your clai::m	
	H:	your clai::m	
	H:	your clai::m	
		I've took it- uh:: I've...	*The dash* indicates a 'cut off' or 'hitch'.
°	P:	°Yeh°	*The degree signs* indicate that the talk they bracket is low in volume.
↑	P:	I said to her ↑ What's thi:s.	*An upward arrow* indicates strongly rising pitch in the word or sound which follows.
↓	A:	It isn't clea::r, from your sta:tement, u-what you're ↓ clai::ming.	*A downward arrow* indicates strongly falling pitch in the word or sound which follows.
wŏrd	A:	Can we no:w (0.3) look at the: (0.2) uh:: (0.7) dispute...	*A dash over a letter* indicates that the sound is long; in this case, 'thee'.
word	A:	It isn't clea::r, from your sta:tement, u-what your'e...	*A dot under a letter* indicates that the sound is short.
.hhh	A:	·t·hhh A:n:d, (·) you're...	*The [hhh]* indicates a breath; preceded by a dot, an inbreath, without a dot, an out-breath. The longer the [hhh] the longer the breath.
(h)	B:	Well that's goo(h)d,	*The [h] in parentheses* within a word indicates explosive breath as in, e.g., laughter and crying.
UC	E:	WELL LET ME SEE HOW THE:: the ball rolls here.	*Upper case* indicates very high volume.

III. Miscellaneous

( )	P:	I mean why should I pay (out) for a brand new dress,	*Single parentheses* indicate that transcribers are not sure about the words contained therein. Empty parentheses indicate that nothing could be
	J:	Like- ( )- someone tied a knot in my stomach.	

G: I jumped outta thē eh seat   made of the sounds. The
     ⌐jumped   speaker-designation column
(L): └(seat,)   is treated similarly

(( )) N: Fine how'r you. ((clipped))   *The double parentheses*
    E: ((cutesy)) I am too.   surround descriptions of the
    B: ((laughs))   talk, as with 'clipped' and
    A: ((clears throat))   'cutesy', or stand in place of an
                                      attempt to transcribe some
                                      utterance as in 'laughs' and
                                      'clears throat'.

6

The Study of Work

Conversational analysis stands as an exemplary achievement, but not necessarily one which can be simply or straightforwardly followed. It is important that we be clear about the kind of example that conversational analysis provides. We ought to add, too, that whilst ethnomethodologists may see conversational analysis as an admirable achievement, this does not commit them to an entirely uncritical respect for it, and some do have more or less serious reservations about aspects of it. The question now, though, is for what is conversational analysis to be admired?

Not because it has provided some general method of sociological inquiry. Nothing could be more mistaken than to think that the key to sociological understanding is to be found by tape-recording and transcribing talk in all kinds of social settings in the hope that by doing so one will have found *the* method of determing how social settings organize themselves. The admirable thing about conversational analysis is not the generality of its methods, but their specificity. Conversational analysis has not provided methods for the analysis of social organization, or even of social interaction, it has provided methods for the analysis of *conversation*.

The argument here requires that we suspend another assumption, whose dispensability might be thought unthinkable, namely that the desire is to construct a cumulative discipline, one in which the results of later studies are continuous with and build upon those of their predecessors. Though we may not have this in sociology it ought to be, surely, what we are aspiring toward. Indeed, if there is something to be said for conversational analysis, then one of the main things might be that it has itself generated a cumulative programme of inquiries and thereby created the possibility of a genuinely cumulative sociology. The results of conversational analysis are indeed cumulative, they have connected up coherently, confirmed and complemented each other, filled out aspects and details of the same frame of reference. The methods have been successful in bringing out the 'built in' structure of a naturally occurring everyday activity, and one which is particularly strategic to social life generally. Thus, conversational analysis has studied language and talk through conversation, and since much of social life is observably conducted through language and talk, even in conversation, then it would appear — if it has succeeded — to have placed in our hands a most fruitful method, one which could be applied very generally. This is, of course, a possibility, but it is not the only one, nor is it that which follows most obviously from ethnomethodology assumptions, nor from conversational analysis's own.

It is at least possible that there will inevitably be discontinuity between ethnomethodology's inquiries. Though there might be cumulation within a given set of inquiries, such as those into the organization of conversation, and though there may be an accumulation of a large body of studies into a wide variety of phenomena, there may be a discontinuity between investigations of one sort of phenomena and those into a different kind. We are, after all, talking about methods of a fair degree of specificity, and those methods which have been productive in conversational studies have been so because they have been specifically contrived to get access to features of conversation's organization. The are not, furthermore, methods which just happen to have succeeded in exposing conversation's in-built structure, but they have done so because they are closely linked with the methods which are used to organize conversation, because they have been (so to speak) tied to the very methods that conversationalists employ to make sense of each other's doings. Thus, for example, a question which naturally arises in conversational inquires is whether we have understood the things which people say correctly? Can there be a proof procedure for establishing that an utterance has been correcly understood? Conversational analysis does not treat this as a distinct problem for itself, but poses it as a problem that must be resolved *within conversational organization itself:* what ways do participants in conversation have of displaying their own understandings or checking out that of others? It is not, after all, as if the possibility that an utterance might have been misunderstood does not matter to conversationalists. It is often important to conversationalists to ensure and establish that understanding has taken place and they have ways of testing for an confirming this: a conversational analyst's claim to have understood utterances can get no stronger support than to be pointed to aspects of the data which establish, for the participants, an unequivocal meaning.

Given that the methods have such a specific connection with the phenomenon under investigation there is no basis for any automatic assumption that they can be extended to other distinct phenomena. It is a real possibility, then, that ethnomethodology must be a pursuit which constantly makes new beginnings. It is not a discipline of new beginnings in a once-for-all sense, but possibly one of perpetual fresh starts. A major change in its topic of inquiries may involve a new beginning, a search for the appropriate and distinctive method for the apprehension of this phenomena. At the very least, there must be continuing awareness of the temptation to import, through the adoption of an already-developed method, a set of inappropriate presumptions about the phenomenon and the proper form of inquiry into it.

That one can contemplate with equanimity the possibility of a discipline which may not progress in the direction of a unified and developed frame of reference may seem unbelievable to someone attached to the frame of reference of Galilean science, but that is because the desire for cumulation within a unified and overarching scheme is such a deep commitment of that frame of reference. However, if someone has withdrawn acceptance from the attitudes of Galilean science, then they have withdrawn it from the deepest and most unquestioned assumptions, as well as from the most superficial and tentative ones. If one is conceiving a programme of inquiries which fall outside the framework of Galilean science, then there is absolutely no reason why one should not conceive of it as lacking the kind of cumulativity that the Galilean programme seeks. That programme seeks for similarity and generality, and in order to do so directs attention away from the specificities and particularities of things. The inquiries of ethnomethodology go in a different direction, looking precisely for the distinguishing and identifying features of phenomena. If we may bring up, again, the link with phenomenology, we can remind that its search was for essential structures, to specify that which makes a phenomenon what it is. It is notable that the expression quiddity (dictionary definition: essence of a person or a thing, what makes a thing what it is) has become increasingly prominent in Garfinkel's later vocabulary, indicating his concern to locate just what it is that gives a phenomenon its identifiable character. Note the continuity, throughout Garfinkel's thought, of basic attention to what gives something its visible, its *recognizable* character.

It is perhaps worth pointing out that, though it may seem that it must, such a conception does not imply the kind of essentialism which involves the supposition that there is some set of inherent characteristics intrinsic to the phenomena which define its being. Given Garfinkel's emphasis on the way in which the sense of social activities is assigned to them, it would go against the whole grain of his thinking to project an inherent identity to anything: the problem must be, how are activities *given* whatever identity they have, how are they *made* different from each other? The object then is to see in whatever ways activities are identified as distinctive, and this can be done without any expectation that some definite or finite collection of such ways must be found.

We must also beware the danger that what we say will be read as rejecting the possibility that there can be anything in common between any two activities. There is no reason always to go from on extreme for another, and to propose looking for the distinctive, identifying features of domains of social actions can be done without intending to insist that one should look for the distinctive, identifying characteristics at the expense, and in disregard of those that are not-so-specific. One may expect to find respects in which there are quite general characteristics of human action, but this can be expected independently of any ambition to have all the significant properties of action derivable from some small number of such general characteristics. Ethnomethodology need not involve itself in asserting the general over the particular, nor affirming the particular against the general, for it can see that the relationship between them is not one of mutual displacement. Thus, as we tried to make clear in the case of the documentary method, general pattern and particular instance were in a relationship of mutual elaboration.

In sociological terms, this involves appreciating just how substantial the reconsideration of the problem of social order has been, just how far it involves allowing the phenomenon to set the problems. One does not begin with a conception of what a sociological problem is, and seek then to see how that problem is resolved in the activities under investigation, one seeks instead to identify the actual issues which are the focus of organizational activity within the setting. Whether or not the production of orderliness within a setting seems to pose or involve problems of 'sociological interest' is neither here nor there for such inquiries, for they are concerned with the real-worldly conditions for the production and reproduction of the recognizable orderliness of activities, *whatever that involves* and *regardless of whether it conforms to received ideas of what are genuine and interesting sociological topics*.

The work of conversational analysis may help in clarifying this. We said that conversational analysis treats conversational order as a production problem. That is, it sought to see how conversational activities assemble themselves in orderly ways. It came to focus its attention on the turn-taking arrangements for conversation, and the ways in which practical organizational solutions are found to questions such as who speaks first?, who speaks next?, when does next take over from current?, how to introduce a particular topic into the flow of talk?, how to make moves toward bringing the conversation to a close? and how to tell that this conversation is at an end, amongst others. It pays attention to these questions because it found that these were the ones around which the step-by-step, utterance-by-utterance putting together of a unified conversation that moved from orderly beginning to orderly closing was organized. It did not approach conversational materials with preconceptions about what they should be analysed for, did not simply use conversational materials, for example, to test hypotheses about whether (say) those with more power spoke more frequently or at greater length but sought, instead, to identify what the organizational problems *produced* and *resolved* in conversation were. Consequently, the methods that conversational analysis identifies are ones which are specific to conversation: they will provide for an orderly taking of turns at talk but they will not enable one to (say) play a game of major league baseball, pilot a 747, win at chess, make a legal argument in court or conduct an experiment in microbiology. If one wants to enquire into how mundane activities other than conversation are conducted then one will have to follow conversational analysis's own example by making a fresh beginning, putting one's own phenomena first. Conversational analysis is exemplary because it aimed to identify the problems and methods constituent of its particular phenomena, to locate materials which would exhibit those problems and methods and to develop a form of analysis which would bring out the problems and methods *constituent* of its particular phenomenon. (In addition, of course, at its best conversational analysis gives examples of the care and integrity with which one can be sensitive to the data one is using, and the scrupulous way in which it can be analysed). Hence, to go about things in the same way that conversational analysis does is not to mimic its specific methods and mode of analysis, but to undertake to articulate, for one's elected phenomena, the very modes of investigation that it *requires*. Investigating mathematical reasoning, for example, is going to be a very different proposition from investigating ordinary conversation, not least because the latter is something that pretty much anyone knows how to do, whilst the former is anything but.

This means that there is no longer a *theoretical* problem of social order, one which is posed on the basis of the discipline's reflection on what is generally required to permit coordinated and stable action. Such a problem is posed from outside the social setting, it is an extrinsic problem which leads the theorist to look at people's activities as though they were organized just to answer the questions the theorist has posed. However, practical social action is not pursued in search of or in order to provide a solution to such questions. Rather than asking, then, what people in society have to do in order to answer the theorist's question, we have to ask what are the constituent problems of order that the practical conduct of the activity involves. Thus, conversational analysis has singled out those organizational problems relevant to carrying on a mutually intelligible conversation. Part of its achievement was to specify the problems to which the methods it identified stood as practical solution. One must acknowledge that in opening up some other topic inquiry one will need to identify its particular, internal problems of order.

Garfinkel is fond of citing an exchange between Fred Strodtbeck and Edward Shils. Strodtbeck was to give a paper on what made the jury a small group. Shils asked why he didn't instead ask what makes the jury a jury. Strodtbeck persuaded Shils that he (Shils) was asking the wrong question. He did not, however, persuade Garfinkel. It is the kind of question that Shils wanted to ask that Garfinkel wants to persist with, and it is questions about what makes activities what they are that have motivated the work of Garfinkel and his students into the organization of work and occupations in the years since the publication of *Studies in Ethnomethodology* in 1967.

SCIENTISTS AT WORK

There is a substantial sociological discipline called the sociology of work but it is, or so Garfinkel would claim, about its alleged subject matter in only the most titular sense. If one was to read the entire literature of the sociology of work, one would find out very little about the work that people actually do, about the work that is the stuff of their daily lives. One will, of course, often find outline descriptions of the work processes of a particular plant or organization, but these are characteristically presented as intro- ductory and background materials before the sociological analysis itself begins. One will not find that the organization of work practices and processes are themselves the objects of sociological inquiry and analysis. For example, take the case which we have mentioned before, of professio- nal–client interaction, particularly the physician–patient relationship. A great deal of sociology has been done on this. Consider Erving Goffman's remarks on the surgical theatre in his essay on Role Distance. There Goffman reports that, in surgery, there is a great deal of byplay between the surgeon and the theatre staff, that the behaviour amongst medical staff there is more like that of Dr. Bob in the Muppet Show or of the Army surgeons in M.A.S.H., with lots of fooling about, than it is like that of those in more usual movie and television versions of operations—tense, serious affairs. However, whilst one thereby learns something about the theatre, one will learn nothing whatsoever from Goffman's essay about surgery itself. One learns nothing whatever about what, after all, the surgical staff are there to do and are doing. The point could be applied generally to studies of medical practice. A great deal has been written about the doctor–patient relationship, much of it from the point of view of the question, who is in control of the encounter, and how is control asserted and maintained? One may, from this, learn much about (let us call it) techniques of interactional control but one will learn nothing whatsoever about the practice of medicine, one will learn nothing whatever about what is involved in giving medical treatment.

These points arise from one of the problems we spoke about early on, that strategies of inquiry sometimes make the phenomenon *disappear* (see Chapter 2) and perhaps can give some indication of why standard methods of sociological investigation do appear to cause this. Suppose one sets out to study something like medicine, but is guided by the desire to look at the encounter in terms (say) the general problems of organizing social interaction and in search of processes which may be found in any kind of social encounter, regardless of the business being transacted there. The fact that one is dealing with a medical encounter becomes a nuisance, something to be disregarded: after all, the things which are essential to it as a medical transaction are irrelevant to it as an instance of social interaction and attention on these peculiarities of it may obstruct and obscure our ability to see in the activity general and generic problems of organizing social action. Consequently, the fact that this *is* a medical encounter, specifically entered into for medical purposes and given its very life by the particularities which it does not share with going to the supermarket or having your shoes shined is almost completely marginal to the analysis. If you want to specify what it is that is distinctively medical about the transaction, you won't be able to get at it that way.

From these reflections emerges an indication of how much conceptions of what it is to look at something sociologically can differ. Consider what is usually thought of as taking a sociological view of something like medicine, science or mathematics. By and large, it is assumed that sociological inquiry must avoid the technical issues involved in them, and that the purpose of sociological inquiry is to show that considerations of a social, rather than a technical, kind enter in to practice. Thus, for example, in a study designed to show mathematics as a cultural system it is deemed important to show that whether mathematical ideas catch on does not just have to do with purely mathematical considerations, but also with the status and power of the person who creates them (status and power being readily recognizable sociological notions). Likewise, in the sociology of science it is thought to be sociological to show that scientific decisions are often influenced by the political, religious, racial and other ideologies of the scientist and that the capacity of one idea to catch on rather than another is the outcome of power struggles amongst groups of scientists. Hence, the main, well established conception of what it is to look at something sociologically is what we will call, in a very loose way, the dependent variable approach. That is, it thinks that to give a sociological account of something is to show how something which appears to be independent of social determinants or influences is actually affected by social factors. We have been talking about this in terms of approaches to science and mathematics, but of course such a conception is every bit as dominant in the study of the arts, where attempts are made to show that music, writing and painting are affected by social forces outside themselves.

Ethnomethodology's notion of what it is to look sociologically is quite different. It begins with the supposition that anything might be a subject matter for sociology, because its conception provides not a demarcation of subject matters but an attitude to phenomena. Looking at something sociologically does not so much involve looking at certain kinds of phenomena as looking at any phenomenon in a certain way. Thus, from ethnomethodology's point of view, establishing that science, mathematics or art might be a proper topic for sociological inquiry does not involve showing that the products of science, mathematics or art are affected by external circumstances, by the environing social structure of the relevant scientific, mathematical or artistic subject matters. On the contrary, looking at those things sociologically involves *looking at them as socially organized phenomena,* involves looking at the doing of scientific inquiry, mathematical reasoning or artistic creation as a socially organized practice. This means, in other terms, examining the ways in which scientific investigation, mathematical calculation and the making of poems are done, in terms of the actions which make them happen. From that point of view, the technical aspects of activity, far from being an irrelevance must be central to all considerations, for it is in their technicalities that such things as art, science and mathematics consist.

Because the study policies which ethnomethodology recommends are so commonly subject to misconstrual, it is only too likely that what we have just argued will be treated as showing a naivete about the relation between science and the real world, in the sence that we are precluding the possibility that (for example) scientific decisions are made under the influence of extra-scientific considerations, out of ideological commitments, political expendiency, religious fanaticism or whatever. No such inference should be drawn, for we are as well aware as any other person, that people do things for reasons other than those they are supposed to entertain. We are, for example, quite well aware that what goes on in the medical transaction may often be anything other than the administration of medical treatment, and that the directions of scientific inquiry may be set by the military interests of the state. Perhaps we should add that we have always regarded conceptions of scientists as wholly unworldly and dispassionate beings as nothing other than comic-strip images and have thus, it seems, been rather less surprised than some of our sociological colleagues seem to be at the fact that scientists can be as greedy, Machiavellian, ambitious, fanatical and ideologically motivated as anyone else.

It is not our object to deny the possibility of such findings, but — as usual — to indicate that we do not regard them as definitive of the form of sociological inquiry, that we do not see the basic or essential purpose of sociological studies into science, mathematics and art to be that of revealing the intrusion of technical irrelevances into technical matters. It should be plain that, from the point of view of a concern with real-worldly practical conduct it is entirely possible to acknowledge that the optimal satisfaction of technical and other-than-technical considerations together will be something people sometimes seek, and that one of the arts of practice is to make technical requirements and resources serve ends decidedly different from those they are technically for. Thus, putting it as crudely as possible, the justification for regarding science as suitable topic for sociological inquiry is that it is a corporate pursuit, something that is jointly organized and collectively carried on, and the fact that science is in the pay or under the influence of the powers (and subject to effects originating in other institutions) arises from that basic fact, not the other way round. The argument about whether science is affected by technical irrelevances simply presupposes that there are technical relevances, and yet sociological analysis cannot specify these. Ethnomethodology sees no reason why the specification of them should be regarded as either outside or beyond the competence of sociological inquiry.

Garfinkel and his collaborators have taken these concerns to the examination of scientific work (though there have been investigations into other kinds of work, too.) There is no fundamental reason why scientific work should be preferred over other kinds for investigation, and in that case they can be chosen because they will serve as well as any other as a place to situate inquiries. There are, however, some reasons for choosing to focus on science, though these are extrinsic to the motivation of the project itself. They are that the question of how to understand the nature of scientific work is a particularly sharp puzzle of interest to the wider world of intellectual debate and because, given the inherently and remorselessly technical nature of scientific work it provides a good opportunity for facing the problem of appreciating the technical character of an activity in a tough, demanding case.

There has been much controversy about science and mathematics in philosophy, and now in sociology, over recent years. But, whilst such arguments may be about and revolve around conceptions of what it is to do science (which may sometimes even insist that science is what scientists do) there is little attempt to see what science, as a matter of working practice, is like. The natural sciences classically are located pursuits. That is, there are places in which they are to be practiced, namely laboratories, and the sciences are there carried out as matters of laboratory work. In a fundamental sense, the conduct of natural science is situated in the laboratory (using that expression to include observatory for the moment) and consists in laboratory work. To understand how laboratory work is organized is, in a fundamental sense, to understand how science is done. And yet, again discussions of science, there is a notable absence of studies of what laboratory work consists in, of how it organizes itself to comprise the *bona fide* practice of science.

The same argument goes for the practice of mathematics. Mathematics consists very much in the construction of proofs, in the conduct of courses of mathematical reasoning, courses which are often carried out collaboratively between mathematicians as they write on paper and blackboards sequences of mathematical argrument, but again in discussions of the nature of mathematics there is the equally notable absence of descriptions of how effective courses of mathematical reasoning are assembled.

Consequently, ethnomethodology's inquiries into science and mathematics are precisely directed toward finding out what laboratory inquiries and mathematical studies consist of as courses of action: what does someone *really have to do* to make a scientific discovery or to establish or retrace a mathematical proof.

This brings us to the last pair of general points that we want to make. These are related and are (1) that social practices, including those of science, maths, art etc. are *incarnate* practices and (2) that the policy is to translate the methodological problems of sociology into problems about the organization of phenomena. These are both ways of recalling philosophical and theoretical controversies to the phenomena that they are about.

Without wishing to make a bland and rather empty contention that the answer to the question 'What is the nature of science?' is that science is what scientists do, there is, nonetheless, something to be said along those lines. Rather than say, though, that science is what scientists do we would want to say that an answer to the question what is the nature of science? must have something to do with what scientists actually do. That does not stand as a bland answer, though, but as a question: just how does the activity of scientists embody the nature of science, in just what ways do the activities of scientists comprise science? There are abundant arguments about the nature of science, and correspondingly about the respective natures of natural and social sciences, but these are, from ethnomethodology's point of view, excessively detached from the examination of the actualities of scientific practice. This is not to say that no reference is made to examples of scientific activity, for various scientific inquiries are held up as paradigm examples of what science is all about, how science is usually done, what science is really like, what science is at its best and so forth. These instances of activity are invoked as ways of advancing a particular conception of what science *amounts to,* but ethnomethology does not seek to develop a parallel, though different conception for itself. It wants, rather, to ask (as usual) about the very possibility of using examples of inquiry to instantiate the nature of science in the first place, about the possibility of being able to see in someones activities (or in records of the same) how science is actually, really, essentially, normally, naturally, properly done. How do activities instantiate the practice of science?

Hence the insistence that phenomena are incarnate. To talk about what science is is to talk in very indirect and deeply unclear ways about what actual people in real world situations are doing, and the first requirement for the clarification of such a problem would seem to be, then, a direct examination of what relevant people are doing. In this case, a look at what is going on in the laboratory or observatory would seem the obvious and needful thing.

Such a proposal might seem to betray the usual methodological naivete of qualitative research, the assumption that one can make generalizations from (at best) a handful of cases, that one could say something about the nature of science on such a limited basis. However, this is where our second policy comes in, for the objective is not to make generalizations in this way, and the interest in looking at the case is not in terms of its potential as a sample basis for generalization. The *methodological* question, what is the relationship between this instance, on the one hand, and such things in general, on the other? gives way to how do the activities going on here connect into, organize themselves into, the business of science?, and this is plainly an *organizational* problem. We have already pointed out that the investigation is not designed to come up with an account of the nature of science, at least in the terms in which such an account would normally be recognized. We have, further, pointed to the way in which the incarnate character of science poses the problem: how do these activities embody science? Hence, inquiry into what goes on in a particular laboratory asks, first of all, what is it about these activities that makes them instances of scientists-at-work, how do these activities exhibit their character as *bona fide* properly and professionally conducted scientific investigations? In answering those questions we are concerned with whatever instance we have in hand, and need make no suppositions as to whether these activities are in any way representative of science-in-general? Any such questions can, must and will be asked at a later point.

Garfinkel and his collaborators have, then, made their inquiries into specific settings of scientific and mathematical activity, have focused on the activities of laboratory work in neuroanatomy, the making of an astronomical discovery, and the work of mathematicians at the blackboard, since it is at these sites that the embodied practice of scientific and mathematical inquiry can be observed. They have, further, placed great emphasis upon the local character of the concerns which the scientists encounter, the way in which their work is tied up with their particular problems and the quite specific circumstances of making a certain sort of inquiry in a particular lab. The argument has been, then, about the unavoidably local character of work, the way in which competent practice of scientific investigation requires more than a mastery of general principles of investigation, but involves also the accumulation of a great amount of much more specific information, some of which is very specific indeed. Also emphasized has been the improvisatory character of the investigative work. Any comic-strip conceptions of scientists as mechanical followers of an explicit, general and invariable method of inquiry cannot withstand the simple evidence of the way in which inquiries are as much worked-up-as-they-go-along as they are done according to rigid, laid down formulae and the concern that scientists show for contriving ways of getting their studies to work out, even when they sometimes have no idea why various practices succeed in the ways they do. Again, it is being pointed out that the nature of science, at least as far as its real work is concerned, is inextricable from the particular considerations of discipline, problem and setting, and that attempts to eliminate these from consideration in order to give a clearer view of the essence of scientific work would be just another example of taking away the walls in order to get a better view of what keeps the roof up.

The insistence of the importance of such local considerations may invite the objection that science is more than goes on in the lab, and that indeed any given lab has its place within much more encompassing social relations: a lab is located, after all, in a discipline. This kind of objection is one we attempted to obviate in our discussion of the convict code, but a second attempt to dispose of it for good and all is probably worthwhile. The investigation into a lab is taken in full recognition of the fact that this is a-lab-in-a-discipline, and that the things that go on in the lab are obviously going to have connections with things outside. Whilst this latter observation may have obvious truth on its side, it is alas lamentably vague. Ethnomethodology is as willing as anyone else to recognize the relevance of 'the outside world' but it does not want to do this by making vague gestures in the direction of whatever lies beyond the walls of the room. It wants, instead, to ask (as usual) about the exact ways in which other-than-local considerations manifest themselves within the locality. It recognizes, too, that the very sense of what is going on within the locality is only apprehensible through a documentary relationship with other-than-local matters, but again wants to ask about the character of definite connections. Thus, for example, it is plainly the case that within an observatory the making of a significant discovery is animated by the realization that one is in the process of doing something significant, and that of course is dependent on one's sense that one is about to become the first to find out something important, something being sought for but not so far found by the rest of the discipline. Likewise, one's sense of what is going on in a neuroanatomy lab will be permeated by one's appreciation as to the standing of this lab within its discipline, and the activities of its participants will be oriented to whether other labs in the same discipline might be working on related problems, might have prospects of making the discovery sought here, are competing for funds and so on. Putting it in a nutshell, ethnomethodology is not focusing upon local social phenomena, but on the localization and embodiment of phenomena.

Science does not just take place in a lab; a lab is, of course, a lab-in-a-discipline and a physics lab will not be like a biochemistry lab, nor will either of those be like the astronomical observatory in important ways, and the way in which things are done will often be discipline specific, they will be ways of doing physics or doing chemistry. They will not be ways of conducting an inquiry for there is no such thing as an inquiry-in-general any more than there is, in the real world, an experiment-in-general. Scientific inquiries are housed in disciplines and an inquiry is, therefore, an inquiry-in-physics or an inquiry-in-astronomy. Indeed, from the point of view of those carrying out the inquiries, they are not doing inquiries-in-physics or inquiries-in-chemistry but are doing inquiries into this or that specific problem in physics or chemistry. These activities are highly specialized and what it takes to do an experiment in one area of a discipline may be such that persons working in other areas of the same discipline could not do it.

Does this mean that ethnomethodology is saying that we can say nothing about science-in-general and that we are condemned to saying just particular things?

To ask this, though, is to stick to the conception we have rejected, of materials as a basis for statistical generalization, to a sample-and-universe conception when an organization-and-local-manifestation conception has been offered instead. The conception that has been rejected makes us think of the detection of regularity as something *post hoc*. It is as if we make an observation of something occurring in a particular case and want then to see if this kind of occurrence is regular, if it occurs in other similar cases. On this basis we need, then, to collect a variety of comparable cases and see if we can, in them, find a regular association between certain things. This is not, however, the conception that is involved here. If we enter a social setting, we do not make a series of observations over a long period of time and then, afterward, draw conclusions about the regularity with which things happen. On entering a social setting we are already on the lookout for things which are routine, regular, commonplace and so forth, and soon after we enter it we will have acquired a sense of which things are regular, routine, unremarkable and so on. We will not have done this, though, by making statistical samples, but by taking note of the kind of activities going on, *the way* in which they are being performed. We would want to suggest that, from ethnomethodology's point of view, the location of regularity has much more to do with demeanour, than with statistical representativeness. How do we, in the ordinary course of things, decide that something is a commonplace occurrence (for it is how we determine matters in the ordinary course of things thaAt ethnomethodology is interested in)? We do not determine that something is commonplace because we have witnessed thousands of occurrences of it. Seeing it once might be enough to establish for us just how commonplace it is. Thus, we might see that something is commonplace because of the way others react to it: they take no notice of it, react to it in ways which express an 'I've seen all this before' attitude. This is what we mean by talking about regularity as a matter of demeanour: how people comport themselves in doing or reacting to something tells us for all practical purposes that this is something they do all the time etc. Let us just add, for emphasis, that we are not at all interested in the statistical soundness of such judgements, for our problem is different: how do people detect, in the organization of locally visible social scenes, regularities and structures?

There is one other respect in which, once again, ethnomethodology turns the problematic around. The usual notion is of standardization-as-explanatory: one explains why someone does something as a product of a general pattern or relationship. Ethnomethodology, by contrast, thinks of standardization-as-achieved. The way we have been putting things might allow the impression that we are saying that everything is unique or idiosyncratic, but nothing of the kind has been said, for there are things which are visibly general or standardized. Comparable with its other strategies, ethnomethodology seeks to examine standardization, the way in which things are standardized. It is, after all, a feature of peoples activities that they seek to organize things in such a way that they can be/will be standardized and the question for us, then, is how to they produce that standardization, how do they *achieve* an arrangement under which such standardization will be possible and actual? For example, it is not just a happenstance feature of science that it is much concerned with devising standard ways of doing things, of locating (for example) sure-fire ways of getting certain outcomes and so on. Indeed, let us note that in the real world of scientific inquiry something which would probably never get a mention in the philosophical and sociological liteature will be of great importance, the working of (so to speak) the scientific furnishings industry will have a role in producing standardization. Laboratories are designed environments, and in their construction and reorganization they will be built to provide for things that, in present and foreseeable conditions of this discipline's practice, will routinely and standardly have to be done there. In setting up the lab as an environment, questions of how to design and equip will involve relations between what suppliers and designers themselves can standardly supply and what practitioners of the discipline will standardly require. People working on and in labs are, then, intimately concerned with questions of how far and in what ways is this lab like other labs? Thus, in setting up a lab questions of how far the relevant parties *want* this lab to possess standard features, and just what those are will be active concerns. Let us avoid charges of environmental determinism, suggestions that lab furnishings might be a fixed constraint on work in labs by pointing out that part of a scientist's competence is to know just how far the fixtures can constrain what he does, to be able to tell when something designed for one use can be adapted for another as opposed to when the way things have been built and fixed with all have to be altered if the work is to be done. Fixtures and fittings can be as much a resource for improvising solutions as anything else. When people are working in labs, then questions about how far what is going on in this lab is like what is going on in others labs animates various aspects of practical concern. Thus, for persons changing their place of employment it is very much a matter of importance as to how far this lab is like the one that he has just left, how far these people do their business in the same way as those others and how far he can carry on working without having to redesign or relearn his working practices.

Another connection in which standardization matters is in regard to being able to do again what others have done before: if one does again an experiment that someone else has done, say, and it does not deliver what they promise it will, then one must start trying to sort out the things involved: could it be, for example, that though it appears that one is doing just the same things as those other people did, that there is something that is different, that one is failing to carry out the experiment in effectively the same way. Or is it, maybe, that after all, the experiment does not work? One may have to start figuring out just what there could be about one's way of doing this experiment that might not, after all, be the same as theirs: how could life in their lab have relevantly differed from life in ours? Another and most important respect in which life in labs is caught up with questions of standardization is in terms of matters of competition and collaboration: labs can work together, and they can be concerned, then, to match up their activities with each other, to keep things closely coordinated and to pass information back and forth so that they will, in relevant respects, be confident they all know about they are doing and that they are doing the same things. Equally, in competitive connections, they will be involved in trying to work out just what the state of play is in other labs, what lines of work are being followed there, whether other people are working in similar directions, whether they have anything like the same techniques, whether — in short — there is any real possibility that these other people may beat them to the discovery that they anticipate.

There are, of course, ways in which a particular lab can stand as representative of science in general or of how this discipline is done. Thus, for example, for lay persons it is possible for them to be taken round a lab and be given some idea of how science (or perhaps chemistry-as-opposed-to-physics) is done. Though there are, for the people who work there or who know anything about the technicalities of chemistry all kinds of important differences between this lab and others in the discipline, the visit to it can provide an all-practical-purposes rendition of what the scientist's life is like: the specifics and technical particularities do not matter to those who have no idea of what is involved in the inquiries. For those who do have competence in the discipline, however, there will be an entirely different battery of considerations as to what makes this (if it is) a choice example of how science is done, and, of course, there will be wholly different considerations for those with technical involvements of one kind in deciding what a piece of work achieves, than there will be for those with different technical engagements. Thus, those who work within a discipline have notions about which are its classical and exemplary studies, about those which canonically display a particularly technique, those which make visible elementary principles of the discipline, those which show the state of the art of technical practice, those which are at the cutting edge of disciplinary growth or at the limits of available technology.

It is not something *external* to it to display the nature of the discipline, for it is a part of the mastery of a discipline to understand these kinds of relationships between its studies. For such matters as, for example, giving instruction to newcomers, making resumés and reports of the state or history of the discipline, organizing conferences on hot issues or chronic problems, devising experiments that will effectively reproduce results and so on it is necessary to look upon inquiries in terms of place within the discipline.

The capacity to see connections between the activities comprising a discipline is *inseparable* from a competence in that discipline. In the final analysis, what happens in laboratories is for those who really know the business to say, and one cannot intelligibly and accurately talk about what goes on in this or that lab without being able to talk shop talk, without being able to talk in the ways that comprise being capable of practice in this discipline and this means that a prominent feature of ethnomethodology's inquiry must be into what is that comprises disciplinary competence. The location of this is rather demanding, since one can only begin to say what that competence is if one can acquire it for oneself. Thus, one finds that Eric Livingston, in order to talk about mathematicians work has to acquire competence in mathematics for himself, that he has to learn *how to do* mathematical reasoning himself in order that he can, in the sense which *to mathematicians* matters, see what they are doing when they are reasoning mathematically. In order to do that, he must be able to follow their courses of reasoning for himself, and that requires that he have considerable competence for his own part. Further, it means that what Livingston finds must, in many ways, remain inaccessible to those who do not have the mathematics themselves. There is a most crucial sense in which saying what the mathematicians are doing cannot be expressed except through their mathematics. In order, for example, to see what a particular mathematical proof achieves then, though one can say in a vernacular sort of way what it amounts to, one cannot really say what it has achieved without understanding the mathematical issues in which it is implicated. In order to see what a mathematical proof achieves, one needs to have some grasp of just what could previously be proved, what kinds of problems were live in the mathematics speciality requiring solution, just how the handling of mathematical technique is involved in providing the proof, just how to tell whether the technique really works, how to see the degree of artfulness and ingenuity in the contrivance and/or use of the technique and so forth. Seeing those things requires, as should be obvious enough, an irreducible understanding of what goes on in maths.

An inquiry into the competence of practitioners and the organization of their professional practice is simultaneously an inquiry into the objectivity of their findings. It is not ethnomethodology's place to provide them with a yardstick against which to assess whether their inquiries are adequate or not, for it is its job to find out what yardsticks are in operation within the practice itself. Just how do people decide what is sound enquiry, when an investigation has reached its conclusion? What is good enough for all practical purposes? What does it take to make something stand up under a real grilling? What are real, as opposed to the apparent, problems in the way of saying this is how it is? The capacity to answer such questions for specific investigations does not involve one in being able to invoke some general standard but in possessing a grasp of how things are done in the discipline, of what kinds of things do and do not matter in making an inquiry, of what the real-worldly, *bona fide* socially sanctioned facts of life in doing say chemistry really are.

Just how loosely or how specifically one must detail what involved in doing something like chemistry not questions inseparable from a knowledge of chemistry. Knowing chemistry as a practitioner is, of course, something other than being able to recite its principles as those are found in textbooks. It is a matter of being able to do chemistry for oneself, of knowing how things are done and knowing (amongst many other things) when something can be done without too much concern for just exactly how it is done, when it can be done in rough-and-ready fashion but will nonetheless serve and when it must be done with the most scrupulous care, just so, or else it will be of no value and will have to be done again. Just how much attention to detail is required is not a question for the sociological methodologist to answer, for it is one that is answered by the chemistry itself, by knowing just what kind of care is required in carrying out a course of action. Similarly, knowing whether findings are sound is a matter of being able to discriminate things that happen all the time but don't really matter and don't count against the worth of what we have got from things that just shouldn't happen if we are doing things right and which suggest that there is something funny going on that we cannot, as good professionals, disregard. It involves, too, being able to tell the difference between things which are first signs of something we have been looking for and have long been expecting to find and things which are simply meaningless manifestations of the working of our machinery, which are — from the point of view of our interests — just so much noise.

Again, one cannot answer questions about whether these particular results are good, are good enough, outside of the practice of a particular discipline and without a grasp of the competence involved in practice of that discipline. Just as one cannot tell what a mathematical proof proves and why it matters without an appreciation of the maths, so one cannot tell whether something is a genuine finding that will stand up to interrogation without a grasp of what counts, within the discipline, as its actual ways of finding out about things, of making them manifest themselves and their properties, of documenting an arguing for their actuality and conclusiveness — and it is, of course, the organization of such things which is the life of the laboratory and observatory. Therefore, and more accessible to the (non-mathematical reader) than the studies of mathematics, there are descriptions of the organization of scientific inquiries which concentrate on the way in which inquirers find and display structures of phenomena. The work of much scientific inquiry is often that of locating and specifying structures of natural phenomena and of finding ways of making those structures visible in the natural occurrences which they underpin. Describing the work of science is, then, at certain points just the same as describing its methods of finding structure in its phenomena. Thus, Michael Lynch has tried to document the ways in which researchers seek to identify neurological structures and make micrographic records of these that are, from their point of view, presentable to the scientific public. One of their problems is to make the distinction between real structures and artefacts of method, to find ways of distinguishing photographs which show what-is-really-there-independent-of-the-method-of-finding-it and what is only-there-because-of-the-procedures-involved-in-making-the-micrograph. He has also examined the ways in which researchers into the behaviour of lizards in their natural environment seek to transfer their patterns of movement to graphs, thus revealing and transfixing the behaviour pattern of the naturalistically observable lizard.

Once again we have given a commentary on the studies rathere than a resumé of them. The strength of Lynch's and Livingstone's work may lie in the fact that they do document in detail the specifics of work in the lab and at the blackboard, but again the important thing in a book such as this is to encourage an appreciation of the reasons why researchers should devote themselves to providing such documentation in the particular manner they do. If we have been at all successful in doing that, then we shall have encouraged readers to look at the details of such studies and perhaps have assisted them in finding more sense in them than otherwise they would have done.

7

What about the Critics?

Once upon a time, one of us was called up by a student. He wasn't one of ours. He was doing a Masters course and had to write something about ethnomethodology. Now he needed some criticisms of it, and his supervisor had told him to ring up and ask what they were. On being told that there were plenty of so-called criticisims but that few, if any, were to be taken seriously he became irritated and abusive. Attempts to explain that it was not so much a matter of having things to say against ethnomethodology, but of making some telling comment that should give a thoughtful and serious ethnomethodologist pause for thought, and that there was precious little which did that, were of no avail. He rang off, obviously disappointed, convinced that there *must be* some good criticisms but that they were being kept from him. We would not like our book to leave the same impression that we are evasively refusing to acknowledge the big holes in the argument. Our opinion of the level of criticism of ethnomethodology has not improved in the years since that telephone call, but we will try to face the main criticisms squarely and to explain why we feel they fail to bite. In part, we have tried to do this throughout our argument by indicating that the *terms* on which ethnomethodology might be prepared to engage in debate with critics are not those in which most would-be critics choose to cast the issues. They, of course, are well satisfied with what they say to the detriment of ethnomethodology, and find much assent to it, but only amongst those who share the same assumptions. Criticisms do not even start to address the issues if they are made on the basis of the very assumptions from which ethnomethodology has withdrawn its attachment. Much criticism is really nothing more than affirmation of difference. Those who make it are pointing out that it is not what they can recognize as sociology, that it is different from what they would ever think of doing. Ethnomethodology, though, is asking whether the assumptions they make are definitive of the field of sociology and to be told that these assumptions are the ones that many, even most, sociologists automatically make does nothing to answer its question: do we *have* to accept these?

Much of the criticism has been anything but open-minded and serious in the way that would be required to allow genuine dialogue. A great deal has been very regrettably *ad hominem,* involving disparagement of the character, integrity and elementary sense of anyone who would take ethnomethodology seriously. Much shows a rather worrying inability to look beyond the most superficial features of ethnomethodology's work, making fun of the writing style of some of it, sneering at the attention paid to dirty jokes, conversations amongst retards, the juicy details of sex-change operations etc. If anyone is to be condemned for triviality we think it is those who judge the merit or interest of thought and argument on the basis of their superficial subject matter, and to whom — seemingly — it never occurs that one might find trite or inconsequential subject matters useful just because they allow the isolation of theoretical, analytical and methodological issues from the passions and presumptions involved in more profound or momentous ones. Moralizing and abuse there is plenty of, pointed and relevant objections, scarcely any.

Attempts at serious criticism do exist, though they are not that numerous and they do not make compelling objections. Two very standard lines are taken and they are, by those who make them, treated as sufficient: if these points are made, it is supposed that no more is needed. They are:

(1) that commitment of an interpretive sociology grounded in the egological approach is necessarily subjectivist and relativist, and that this is wholly unacceptable; and

(2) that the explanations of social phenomena which ethnomethodology provides are necessarily inadequate since they preclude, by virtue of their form, identification of the causal factors which do explain social behaviour. Concretely, such criticisms allude to the objective determinants of social action, which they identify with such things as class position, gender, ethnicity and/or location in other kinds of power relationship.

Far from bringing any reasonably open-minded ethnomethodologist to see the error of his ways, these arguments are apt just to confirm the conviction that the critics have, once again, missed the point. Such criticisms betray the mistaken impression that ethnomethodology is broadly the same kind of thing as other sociologies, with much the same objectives and strategy. As we have tried to indicate, ethnomethodology is not directly comparable with those rival theories, and we have remarked that the interests of the two parties are tangential. This is the moment to give this point maximum emphasis.

NAIVE? SIMPLISTIC?

If ethnomethodology were pursuing the same goals as other theories, then it would indeed be naive if it neglected important structural determinants of conduct; but the fact that it makes no mention of these does not show it has left them out, only that mention of them is irrelevant to the issues in hand. Ethnomethodology's studies relate to other sociological studies in being *foundational*. That is, they enquire into those things on which other approaches to sociology found themselves, but into which they do not themselves inquire. This is most marked in relation to ethnomethodology's topic of investigation, the organization of daily life. This is not an object of sociological attention *as a phenomenon in its own right* except in ethnomethodology. The availability of the world of daily life as the scene of sociological practice is something sociology typically takes for granted and does not further inquire into. To take a prominent instance, the fact persons have at their disposal the mastery of a natural language is a presupposition of writing and reading sociology and of making its inquiries with its subjects, yet sociology of language is at best a marginal area of sociology and that is hardly notable for its examination of the nature of natural language mastery. In this and many other ways, then, sociological inquiries require acceptance *without reflection* of the existence of an already ordered organization of social affairs, *within which* it is meaningful to pose the questions that they ask and to recommend the methods with which they intend to answer them. Their modes of investigation and analysis simply do not raise the issue of how everyday orderliness is made available, nor how it is that this availability ensures the effectiveness of favoured methods of inquiry.

In saying these things it will most likely seem that we are making criticism of 'constructivist' sociology, that we are indicting it for a failure to reflect on its own foundations. This seems to be the way that many sociologists take ethnomethodology's arguments, primarily as criticisms of their way of doing things, and this is perhaps why they respond so sharply to them. Their criticism of ethnomethodology is perhaps undertaken in defence of their own position. However, a failure to examine the foundations of ones own undertaking is by no means to be thought necessarily a failing. If one is to engage in an undertaking, then things must be taken as given, and one cannot both carry on the undertaking *and* step back from it to reflect upon it. Thus, the things which constructivist sociology does not reflect upon are things that it cannot reflect upon, not as long as it retains a commitment to its project: reflection on its own foundations would require it to distance itself from just those commitments. Ethnomethodology does not need to mount its own criticisms of constructivist sociology, it can simply take note of those which constructivist sociologists make of each other. It is *they* who indict each other's work quite savagely and severely, who point out the gross inadequacies of each other's theories, and some are so disenchanted with the general state of sociological theory they complain that there is nothing really worthy of the name theory in the whole discipline. Similarly, it is constructivist sociologists who engage in mutual disparagement over methods: protagonists of quantitative methods are often utterly dismissive of qualitative studies, and those who practice the latter are often correspondingly contemptuous of quantification. In terms of specific studies, constructivist sociologists are quite willing to expose the fundamental methodological vulnerabilities of each other's work. This, at least, gives ethnomethodology the opportunity to argue that it can undertake examination of the foundations without risking the disturbance of a settled and stable structure.

Ethnomethodology is not bidding to do, as well or even better, the things that constructivist sociologists are aiming to do; its problems and those that sociologists usually address are, to repeat, at a tangent. Ethnomethodology's inquiries characteristically will end where those of the others normally begin, i.e. will be into what they have assumed to start with. Thus, at the most elemental level, sociological theory and method asks how may we capitalize on the availability of an observably regular world of daily life? whilst ethnomethodology asks how it is that an observably regular world is there to be capitalized on? Rather than priding ourselves on the fact that we can make more sophisticated sense of the social world around us we might inquire into our capacity to make sense at all. These questions come before those which sociology usually asks, and some practical solution to them is presupposed in standard inquiries.

This indicates the suitable answer to criticisms of the second sort that we specified above, those which allege that ethnomethodology cannot adequately explain courses of action since it does not identify the structural constraints which are determinants of action. *If* the explanation of action through the influence of structural determinants *is* the objective of sociology, it is not that of ethnomethodology. Hence, argument about whether ethnomethodology has the resources to explain why people act in the ways they do is an utter irrelevance.

Going right back to our discussion of Alfred Schutz, we pointed out that Schutz was trying to see how *any* regularity in social life could be found, and that he began by suspending an assumption that others had made, that activities have intrinsic sense. Schutz did not do this in order to deny that actions make sense, but in order to show as problematical something which had not hitherto been seen as such, namely that actions *do* make mutually intelligible sense.

Schutz nowhere provided a causal account of anyone's actions, for his own task was that of describing *the process of interpretation* through which it was possible to look for and find explanations of why people act as they do. Garfinkel took up Schutz's problematic, but treated it as much more of an empirical problem, calling for the detailing of the ways in which people make mutual sense of each others actions, the methods they use to recognize each others pursuits for what they are. Garfinkel does not ask how he, as ethnomethodologist, might identify the correct causal explanation of a given action or practice because *his question* is about the ways in which matters of fact, causality, determination are established within society, how people find that this is so, that this causes that, that this explains the other. As far as Garfinkel's strategy is concerned, sociologists findings about the structural determinants of action are one further example of the way in which people in society locate causes and explanations, and as such are as fitting a topic as any other for his own inquiries. It should be made absolutely clear that Garfinkel is *neither* denying that one can locate objective determinants of action *nor* proposing his own versions of what those determinants are, in contradiction to those that other theories identify. Garfinkel is concerned with the *organizational properties of mutual intelligibility* and in order to tackle that problem one can maintain a simple indifference toward and between structural theories of the causation of action.

These same points bear upon attempts (which we think are usually patronizing) to grant ethnomethodology some legitimacy by including it within some allegedly more comprehensive master scheme, attempting to allow that ethnomethodology has merit, but that this is limited and complementary to that which other sociological approaches have. The tendency is, then, to see that ethnomethodology is a kind of micro-sociology, which may adequately identify the face-to-face and local determinants of action, but which cannot specify the structural conditions which occasion the face-to-face encounter, which generate the properties of the local setting and which provide the cultural resources which animate and structure the encounter. These arguments suppose that the *entire* project of sociology is with identifying the determinants of action, and that ethno-methodology has succeeded in identifying some of these, when ethno-methodology is not looking for structural determinants at all. Ethno-methodology's inquiries are *exclusively* concerned with the ways in which actions are interrelated to produce and reproduce a recognizable order of everyday affairs, with the way in which *from within the local setting* the presence of an environing and constraining social world may be made manifest, with the ways in which the dependence of events in the here-and-now can be discovered to be consequentially dependent upon things happening far away, long ago, in the world at large, etc. As we argued in connection with the documentary method it cannot conceive a separation of the face-to-face situation and the social structure since these are mutually elaborative: one cannot establish what is really happening in a face-to-face encounter except by recognition of it as an-encounter-in-a-structure. Consequently the treatment of ethnomethodology as a micro-sociology involves its placement in a dualism which it maintains is untenable.

We can, of course, accept that it is possible that ethnomethodology's efforts to get away from the dualism of interaction and structure may have been unsuccessful (though we know of no arguments which recognize that the attempt has been made, let alone which have set out to show why they do not succeed) and that it is also possible that it does need a set of structural categories to fill it out, but we cannot accept that this would be because of a naive disregarding of the role of objective social structures and structural determinants of action of which it is accused.

The disagreement is, in a way, over who it is that has the other surrounded? That is, it is a question of who is taking the more general approach? The critics think they are, for reasons indicated: they think that the task is to build up a system which contains all the determinants of action, and since they are confident they have already identified some of these they are sure that ethnomethodology can at best only identify some others. Therefore, if there is anything to ethnomethodology, the most it can do is to tell part of the story. What really puzzles the critics then, of course, is ethnomethodology's seeming refusal to recognize that this must be so, its seeming and astonishing indifference to, disregard of, perhaps even ignorance about the import of such structural considerations as class and power.

If such critics were to attempt to look at ethnomethodology in its own terms, rather than insisting on seeing it through the spectacles of their own approach, they might notice that what ethnomethodology persistently attempts to do is to describe *interpretive practices,* rather than to identify the causes of actions. In short, ethnomethodology does not think of itself as telling either the whole or a part of the story, but of trying to examine the ways in which *any* story might be told, with the ways in which stories are projected and interpreted as intelligible, coherent, plausible, demonstrably correct and so forth, and claims about the real-world, demonstrably determinant role of observable social structural factors provide further occasions for examination of accounting practices, not the moment for the adoption of one or other view about what the real determinants are. In that sense, ethnomethodology thinks that it has the more general set of preoccupations. Its critics are arguing about the nature of the best theory of the social world, whilst ethnomethodology is concerned with the possibility that the social world can be theorized at all.

SUBJECTIVIST? RELATIVISTIC?

The other main accusation is that ethnomethology is subjectivist and relativistic. The terms in which the accusation is made indicates, clearly enough, that the issue is meant to be cast in philosophical terms, and that general conceptions of the nature of reality are to be pitched against each other. The accusers usually want to hold that social reality is an objective reality, something existing independent of our thoughts and experience and they suspect, may even be confident, that ethnomethodology is attempting to deny these things. Even if it were to disavow any such intention, the critics would perhaps want to maintain that no matter what it says, it does in effect treat social reality as something which has a subjective character and encourages the idea that reality is what anyone says it is.

It would be hasty to assume that answers to such questions lie within ethnomethodology's competence. The very notions of objective and subjective, and of their methodological implications, are matters of continuous debate within philosophy and no firm, agreed answer is to be found there. There are those who think that objectivity can be had — has even already been attained in some areas of human thought and should be sought and attained everywhere else as quickly as possible. Others think that objectivity cannot be had, that it is mere illusion, and that we should be grateful for this. Of course, even amongst those who agree with each other about the possibility or impossibility of objectivity there is not that much consensus about just what it is that we can or cannot have, what it is that would give objective results their objectivity, what methods are necessary to the attainment of objectivity and so forth. On its own view of itself, phenomenology has avoided the dualism of object and subject, absolute and relative. Its critics may well disagree with this but that does not clinch any arguments.

It is quite reasonable, therefore, for the sociologist to adopt a pragmatic attitude to the selection of philosophical premises, looking to the investigative possibilities that they open up, rather than to the metaphysical certainty that they can claim. In presenting a comparison of the pretheoretical philosophical elections of Parsons and Schutz, Garfinkel was concerned to display them as a set of irreducible alternatives: one could, quite reasonably, choose one or the other, though the consequences of making a choice would be far-reaching. Phenomenology is no more nor less debatable than any other philosophy but it does, in Garfinkel's view, show an awareness of the matters that he wants to attend to that other philosophies do not. Since philosophical certainty cannot be had, sociological fertility may as well be the test.

The point is, though, to use phenomenology to derive a *methodology*, not an ontology, i.e. a doctrine about what the world is really made of, the advantage being that adoption of it enables one to get away from some questions which have invariably preoccupied sociology and to look at others which it has not been able to take up. Thus, for example, the adoption of the device of bracketing allows one to get away from asking whether things really are the way members of the society say they are in order that one may examine what members of the society say they are and how they satisfy themselves that things are that way. Such a method does not commit one to supporting the claims that the members of society make, endorsing common sense or anything like it, but precisely allows one to adopt an attitude of neutrality in controversies about the correctness or otherwise of common sense.

Criticism of the egological approach as necessarily subjectivist and relativist arises from a tendency to read ontological claims much too quickly into steps which are taken for methodological reasons. These steps are not taken in order that the world of daily life, as known through common sense, may be identified as the ultimate locus of reality and the final focus of sociological inquiries. Indeed, it is just these attempts to lay out in advance what the scope and subject matter of sociology *must* be that ethnomethodology declines to make. What social reality is, and what can be said about it is something for investigations to determine, and the most that contentions about this can achieve at the present stage of things is an opening up of topics for investigation. Hence, the appeal of phenomenology is not because it necessarily has succeeded in obviating the dualisms which it aims to overcome, but because it shows that one does not need to begin by confining ones conception of how sociology can be initiated within the boundaries provided by those self-same dualisms which are so commonly allowed to demarcate sociology's territory. The test of whether following along lines indicated by phenomenology was the right decision is whether this enables one to get at the thing one aims to study, whether it does enable one to get to grips with the organization of the world of daily life without losing sight of its commonplace, everyday, familiar character.

As far as the pursuit of objectivity goes, the issue very much depends on what you think objectivity is. One point of view is that objectivity is very clearly and procedurally defined: it requires recognition of and faithful adherence to a set of rules of inquiry, taking notice only of the things that can be handled by those methods. If a phenomenon cannot be treated in terms of those methods then it should be disregarded. If that *is* objectivity, then some of us might want to say we do not want it. If objectivity means that we cannot be interested in many things about social life because they cannot be studied in certain ways, then since it is the characteristics of social life that draw our attention in the first place we shall prefer to keep our interest in the topic and decline to follow the method, to scarifice objectivity in favour of faithfulness to the phenomenon.

However, we should not be too eager to accept that those who would define objectivity in terms of a specific set of methods have given an accurate definition. Objectivity is often employed as an honorific and to say of someones inquiries that they are objective is to say that they put the object before the subject, that they are more concerned to ensure that the phenomenon is adequately and correctly described, that the inquiries are dispassionate rather than dominated by the preferences and prejudices of the inquirer. On such a conception, it seems fair to say that ethnomethodology's inquiries are as objective in intent as anyone's in sociology, and that they may even be more objective in achievement than others. It certainly goes much further than other sociologies in giving primacy to the phenomenon and insisting that inquiries be directed toward revealing its properties. To ethnomethodology, the attempt to contain investigations within a preconceived conception seems often to result in forcing the data into formats which cannot satisfactorily contain it, seeking to capture phenomena through data that does not seem to show the properties but which can be handled conveniently by preferred methods. This appears to involve obscuring or distorting the properties of the things being studied and that is hardly consonant with the meaning of objectivity.

If objectivity involves a devotion to the objectification of the phenomena, for the accurate specification of the data and the development of techniques that are best designed to expose the nature of the phenomena, being most accurately aware of the danger of imposing alien preoccupations on it, then ethnomethodology can claim to show at least as strong a commitment to this as anyone. It may appear that it is somewhat haphazard and slapdash in its work because it does not have the kind of concern for methods of data collection which are so prominent in the methodological literature, but this highlights another difference between the two approaches. From ethnomethodology's point of view, standard methods show an excessive preoccupation with the question of how you are to get your data in the first place, and a very limited concern with what you are going to do with it once you have assembled it. This does not lead ethnomethodology to think that one can be indifferent to problems of data collection, for one needs to be as scrupulous about that as anything else. However, *at this stage of things* one does not need to go to any great or complicated lengths to collect data. *At this stage of things* one can often take data that is quite arbitrarily chosen, and, given that, one might as well take data which can be easily and conveniently collected, which is used just because it is to hand. Though this is generally the case, this is not always so. In order to collect certain kinds of materials one must go to exacting lengths to acquire it: thus some of Garfinkel's students have had to take qualifications in mathematics and law in order that they may talk about mathematical and legal topics. The casualness about data collection is, then, only apparent, for it results from stringent thinking about the relevance of data. If one wants to examine certain kinds of problem, does it matter what kind of data one uses? Is a specific kind required or will more or less anything do? The answer, of course, depends on the problem: in some cases, only a certain kind of material can possibly serve, in others virtually anything will serve equally well.

Insofar as the analysis of data is concerned, though, ethnomethodology has imposed on itself the most stringent discipline, the discipline of coming to terms with the data, *whatever that is*. Its ways of working do not allow anyone to avoid the difficulties the data may pose in favour of achieving a principled solution to a problem. Whatever problem may lead one to choosing certain kinds of data, if it proves that the data — once collected- — makes the solution of that problem difficult, those difficulties cannot be set aside, the data must be worked through and the bearing of it on the initial problem must be appreciated, even if it means a thorough revising of ones ideas about what a problem can be.

If objectivity is thought to involve the creation of reproducible results and materials, then again ethnomethodology has made sterling efforts at it. Though the objectification of phenomena is not to be given such a prominent position that it requires the distortion of phenomena in an attempt to objectify things which cannot be objectfied, insofar as that is compatible with faithfulness to the phenomena, then it is to be sought. Thus, ethnomethodologists have sought to make their data available for the direct inspection of the sociological community, and to make as explicit as possible the steps by which they have investigated it, in order that colleagues may see how conclusions were derived from the material and may replicate the analysis for themselves. If talk about hard data is to be engaged in, then some ethnomethodological studies, especially those of conversational analysis can, we think, be said to be harder than anything else in sociology. The data is initially gathered by a recording machine, and is them transcribed as carefully as can be and in such a way as to retain very many of the features of the talk as recorded. The carefully prepared transcript is available to other researchers and the tape itself can often also be obtained and heard by them. The research report will contain the relevant excerpts of transcript which justify its arguments and readers can see just how the arguments about the data correspond to its actual features. In the direction of making both the materials and methods of study publicly available and replicable, conversational analysis seems to go at last as far as anyone else in the discipline.

The commitment to the primacy of the phenomenon should limit and override the requirement to objectify, but not because it weakens a commitment to objectivity, for it is itself a form of commitment to objectivity. Its purpose is to place the requirement to see the object *for itself, as it has been found in experience* at the forefront and to provide an inhibition on the tendency to let a set of preconceptions take over, to let the methods be adapted to the nature of the phenomenon, not the other way around. It would be unfaithful to the phenomenon if one were to seek to objectify something that connot be objectified.

The foregoing remarks mislead if they suggest that the purpose of ethnomethodology's inquiries is to enable it to call itself objective. In important ways, it really does not matter whether one calls the inquiries one makes objective, scientific or anything else. What matters is the inquiries themselves, not the titles under which they are done. Our point here is that if people are to bandy about claims of superior objectivity or rigour then these are not to be regarded as unarguable, nor are they even to be accepted as expressing the only conceivable ideas of objectivity or rigour. We have, then, insisted that ethnomethodology can argue that it is just as rigorous and just as objective as any other sociology if not more so. Though there are important differences in the respective conceptions of rigour and objectivity which ethnomethodologists and other kinds of sociologists hold, it should not be thought that these are entirely distinct. In terms of objectivity, at least, it can be argued as we have tried to do that ethnomethodology can satisfy the critic's conception of objectivity as reasonably as its own.

Ethnomethodology suspects that sociology-at-large over-values the importance of adequate philosophical and theoretical preparation and grossly underestimates the difficulty of translating programmes into practice. Theorizing is the high prestige activity, and data collection and analysis of low esteem, desirably the kind of thing that can be done in an entirely mindless and mechanical way. Thus, the business of collecting and analysing data is often farmed out to hired hands (as Julius Roth called them), with the consequence that theorizing is often conducted out of contact with and through little concern for the problems of operationalization. It is taken for granted that if the theoretical orientation can be clarified, then the problem of researching and analysing social settings in terms of it will be negligible. Hence, ethnomethodology's critics are apt to regard its labouring over the difficulties of analysing a small amount of inconsequential data as utterly footling, and to think that all that can be virtually dismissed in order to prevent concern with small things obscuring the big and tough problems. However, ethnomethodology does not labour with small fragments of data in order to avoid big problems, but because it finds small investigations are hard enough to push through with any care for the problems they pose.

Ethnomethodology's own experience, then, teaches it that making investigations which are empirically sound is a very tough business, and that those who imagine that obstacles to investigation will be easily resolved are often showing their own lack of acquaintance with the difficulties of actual inquiry and, indeed, their own insensitivity to the persistent problems which afflict sociological investigations of the standard kind. Criticism from such sources as to the misdirected character of ethnomethodology's inquiries cannot be accepted. Someone who has not tried to grapple with those problems is in no position to say how trivial or easy they are.

In sum, then, whilst it is wholly possible that ethnomethodology is on the wrong track, the criticisms so far outlined provide no real reason for thinking that it is so. They require, for their force, acceptance of assumptions which are up for debate or, indeed, the treatment of disputable issues as though they have been unequivocally settled. Rather than showing ethnomethodology the error of its ways, they often betray rather drastic misconceptions as to what those ways are.

Who could suppose that ethnomethodology was impervious to criticism? We cannot see any criticisms that significantly touch it, but there are some which do show some comprehension of and sensitivity to its concerns and which are, therefore, aware of places at which it is vunerable. The criticisms which do this have tended to come from inside. Let us say a little about one or two of these sore spots.

ONE MORE STEP?

Since ethnomethodology itself has the policy of pushing things as far as they can go in the direction of an inevitable stopping point, then it is of course fair game for inspection in the same terms. Has it gone as far as it might in the direction of radical (i.e. to-the-root) examination of its own assumptions? Alan Blum, Peter McHugh and their colleagues have argued that it has not, and have developed an approach of their own, which they call Analysis, which originates in an Heideggerian rather than Husserlian inspection of foundations. Martin Heidegger saw many of the presuppositions of thought being contained in the language, and he sought to expose these through a kind of etymological analysis of the meaning of words, revealing in the process the kind of commitments that people would be unaware that they had made. Blum, McHugh and co-workers use a very similar method to bring to light auspices under which ethnomethodology operates, and to show that these are not perhaps quite so distinctive from those of positivism as it would like to think. Both ethnomethodology and other kinds of sociology are being accused of a kind of bad faith, but of a moral rather than a theoretical sort. Rather than obscuring theoretical assumptions they are seen as misrepresenting as theoretical and empirical problems what are in fact problems of community and authority, of seeking sounder sociological investigations when what is needed is a reconstruction of the whole form of intellectual life, of pursuing methodological objectives when an authentic relationship with others is what should be sought.

DATA—WHO NEEDS IT?

Again the question may be asked, though in a less far-reaching way than it is by Blum and McHugh: how far has ethnomethodology removed itself from positivist type assumptions? Though it may, in certain ways have disso-ciated itself from them, there is at least the risk that it will revert to them in practice and, in particular, that the desire to objectify phenomena may lead it to betray its own assumptions. The desire to provide and analyse data may take on a life of its own, such that the nature of the phenomenon under inquiry may be forgotten. The availability particularly of recording equip-ment, such as tape recorders, videos and cameras may seem to provide us with data, with transcripts, films and photographs, and it may be that the insistence on working with data of this kind may lead to a constricting of the phenomena available to study, that one may take the recordable/transcrib-able, filmable and photogenic character of phenomena as the prime consideration in deciding whether or not they may be studied. It is, however, a good question as to what, exactly, *the* data is, and there may be a mistaken identification of it with the concrete materials, such that (say) the transcript is taken as the data. However, it may equally well be argued that the data is not the transcript, tape, film or photograph at all, that data is the common-sense understandings and interpretive procedures of persons and that it is these which are being examined: they are not things which can be made concrete, and which are certainly not made so through objectifica-tion in transcript, tape etc. The data, on this line of thought, are the reactions, interpretations and assumptions of people, and objectifications in the form of tapes etc. are useful in enabling us to become aware of and to articulate assumptions, thoughtless interpretive practices an so on, but it would be a reification to give them status as the only permissible starting points for inquiries.

Such a focusing upon the data may also lead to investigators losing sight of the elemental fact of research, that the materials are themselves productions, that they have been produced by research practices and data collecting and analysing techniques and that, therefore, their standing as an objective record of what was really said/visibly done is no less dependent upon accounting practices than is any other objectification of social settings. Thus, the work of seeing order and pattern in a transcript, video or photograph may be something made possible by the capacity to replay, halt, write down, and inspect it closely over and over again, and in that respect the relationship between what the researcher sees in the data and what was/would be noticed by social actors living in real-time situations which cannot call back a recording of what was just said may become problematic. Howard Schwartz, in the paper from which we have taken the heading of this section, points to the way in which the-real-order-of-a-queue-for-service might be something resistant to recording, that the distribution of turns amongst people waiting to apply for visas is not something that can be captured by a photograph of them while they wait. They are sitting in chairs around the room and are not placed according to order of arrival, and that fact may give rise to unresolvable questions as to who was before whom. Likewise, Garfinkel complains about the dangers of treating materials as docile, as regarding them as resources which the researcher may freely manipulate in pursuit of his own interests, thus obsfuscating the real worldly and intractable character of the phenomena they may be intended to portray.

We mention these two objections just to show that far from being a self-admiring and uncritical affair, ethnomethodology is in truth most self-critical, always demanding that its own work at least meet the requirements it would set for anyone else and setting it as stiff a set of standards of achievement as it can.

CONCLUSION

Let us close by identifying, briefly, a few leading characteristics of ethnomethodology's work. It is tempting to try to summarize ethnomethodology in a conventional way, in a way which would make it more easily comparable with other sociological theories by saying, for example, that it has an active, creative conception of the social actor (rather than a passive, reactive one), that it emphasizes reality as subjective rather than objective and so on, but these are the ways of thinking which form the discourse in which it does not want to participate. The way in which we would want to identify its distinctive features are, then, in terms which point to the characteristics of its best studies, such as:

(1) A concern with primordial relations. It is not concerned with those kind of connections constructivist theories attempt to make, but with the kind of connections which come *before* those, the making of which is presupposed in the inquiring and reasoning constructive analysis does. Thus, rather than being concerned to ask what connections the data might show, it wants to ask by what procedures the data was put together in the first place, what connections have assembled it as a corpus of data?

(2) A fixation on readily visible orderliness. The aim is to take note of the orderliness that anyone might identify, to see the kind of orderliness which is routinely recognized and attended to by those who inhabit the daily round. There is no desire to find orderliness other than could be readily recognized, to see patterns that others would not detect, but to see how that readily recognized, commonplace orderliness is produced and recognized.

(3) A preoccupation with production problems. Rather than looking for reasons for the existence of social practices, it occupies itself with the identification of the ways in which practices are produced and reproduced, with identifying the things that people actually do to bring about the states of affairs that we find confronting us, and the practices which make such findings, with how people discover, characterize and display the unremarkable orderliness that the world of daily life exhibits.

We could extend this list, but there is no immediate need for it, since its point is simply to show that, even if the concerns of ethnomethodology are wrong-headed, at least they are distinctive.

Suggestions for Further Reading

CHAPTER 1

An impression of the difficulties in communication between ethnomethodologists and other sociologists can be gained from Richard Hill and Katherine Crittenden (eds), *The Purdue Symposium on Ethnomethodology*, Institute Monograph No. 1, Institute for the Study of Social Change, Purdue university, 1968.

A concise account of Husserl's views are given in part one of *Husserl and the Search for Certitude* by Lesek Kolakowski, Yale University Press, 1974, and among the more accessible expositions by Husserl himself are *The Paris Lectures*, The Hague, Martinus Nijhoff, 1964, and *Cartesian Meditations*, The Hague, Martinus Nijhoff, 1960.

The third volume of *Collected Papers*, Martinus Nijhoff, 1966 brings together the writings of Alfred Schutz on phenomenology. His reflections on the foundations of Max Weber's sociology are in *The Phenomenology of the Social World*, London, Heinemann, 1976. A useful selection is Helmut Wagner (ed), *Alfred Schutz on Phenomenology and Social Relations*, Chicago, University of Chicago Press, 1970, and Wagner has also authored *Alfred Schutz, An Intellectual Biography*, Chicago, University of Chicago Press, 1983.

An idea of different views than ethnomethodology's as to what pheno-menology might mean for social science can be gained from George Psathas (ed), *Phenomenological Sociology*, New York, Wiley, 1973, and from Maurice Natanson (ed), *Phenomenology and the Social Sciences* (2 vols), Evanston, Northwestern University Press, 1973; and an example of Natan-son's own work is *Phenomenology, Role and Reason*, Springfield, Charles Thomas, 1974. Peter Berger and Thomas Luckmann's *The Social Con-struction of Reality* was first published by Doubleday, New York, in 1966.

CHAPTER 2

Felix Kaufmann's analysis of the rules of scientific method in sociology is contained in his *The Methodology of the Social Sciences*, New Jersey, The Humanities Press, 1958. Garfinkel's general approach to theorizing is shown in his 'Some sociological concepts and methods for psychiatrists', *Psychiatric Papers*, Vol. 6, Summer 1956, pp. 181–195. His views on the importance of phenomenology to sociology are given in 'When is sociology phenomenological?', *The Annals of Phenomenological Sociology*, Vol. 2, 1977, pp. 2–16. Aaron V. Cicourels most influential works are *Method and Measurement in Sociology*, New York, The Free Press, 1964, and *The Social Organisation of Juvenile Justice*, London, Heinemann, 1976. John Heritage's *Garfinkel and Ethnomethodology*, Oxford, Polity Press, 1984, is a good introduction to the whole range of Garfinkel's thought.

CHAPTER 3

Talcott Parsons's main writings are *The Structure of Social Action*, New York, The Free Press, 1968, and *The Social System*, London, Routledge & Kegan Paul, 1951. He gives a memoir of his intellectual development in 'On building social systems theory', *Daedalus*, Vol. 99, 1970, pp. 826–881. Our main source for Garfinkel's interpretation of Parsons is his Ph.D. thesis, *The Perception of the Other: A Study in Social Order*, Unpublished thesis, Harvard University, 1952. Some of the disruption experiments are reported in 'A conception of and experiments with trust as a condition of stable, concerted actions', in O. J. Harvey (ed), *Motivation and Social Interaction*, New York, Ronald Press, 1963, pp. 187–283. The origins of the term ethnomethodology are recounted in the *Purdue Symposium*, reprinted in Roy Turner (ed), *Ethnomethodology*, Harmondsworth, Pen-guin, 1974.

Alfred Schutz's approach to the foundations of interpretive sociology is worked out in *The Phenomenology of the Social World*, in the first two volumes of *Collected Papers*, The Hague, Martinus Nijhoff, 1962–1964 and in *The Structures of the Life World* (with T. Luckmann), London, Heinemann, 1974. The development of his philosophy towards Husserl's phenomenology is described in *Life Forms and Meaning Structures*, London, Routledge & Kegan Paul, 1982. The correspondence between Schutz and Parsons is collected in R. Grathoff (ed), *The Theory of Social Action*, Bloomington, Indiana University Press, 1978.

CHAPTER 4

This chapter draws on Harold Garfinkel's *Studies in Ethnomethodology*, New Jersey, Prentice-Hall, 1967, and the account of the convict code is taken from D. Lawrence Wieder's *Language and Social Reality*, The Hague, Mouton, 1974. The essence of Wieder's study is excerpted in Roy Turner (ed), *Ethnomethodology*, pp. 144–172. The example of the coding problem is from Bruce A. Katz and W. W. Sharrock, 'Eine Darstellung der Koderiens', in Elmar Weingarten, Fritz Sack and Jim Schenkein (eds), Berlin, Suhrkamp, 1976. The discussion of the astronomical discovery draws on Harold Garfinkel, Michael Lynch and Eric Livingston, The work of a discovering science construed with materials from the optically discovered pulsar, *Philosophy of the Social Sciences*, Vol. 11, 1981, pp. 131–158. A neglected and underestimated paper which gives some substance to claims about sociologys dependence of common sense and natural language is Edward Rose, 'The English record of a natural sociology', *American Sociological Review*, Vol. 25, 1960, pp. 193–208.

The collection edited by Turner contains a good and varied selection of ethnomethodological writings, as do the Weingarten, Sack and Schenkein collection and George Psathas (ed), *Everyday Language*, New York, Irvington Press, 1979. This collection contains Melvin Pollners 'Explicative transactions: making and meaning in traffic court'.

CHAPTER 5

The unpublished lectures of Harvey Sacks were generously provided to inquirers in mimeographed form for many years, but these have not yet been published nor, as far as we are aware, is there any immediate prospect of the release of even a selection. These are undoubtedly the main source for getting a proper sense of what Sacks was up to, and only the faintest idea of the quality and range of his thought can be obtained from the published papers and the few lectures which have been printed in collections such as Psathas (ed), *Everyday Language*, New York, Irvington Press, 1979; Max

Atkinson and John Heritage (eds), *Structures of Social Action*, Cambridge, Cambridge University Press, 1984. Don Zimmerman and Candace West (eds), *Language and Social Interaction*, Numbers 3 and 4 of *Sociological Inquiry*, Vol. 50, 1980. A large sample of writings in conversational analysis may be found in these sources, and in David Sudnow (ed), *Studies in Social Interaction*, New York, The Free Press, 1972, John Gumperz and Dell Hymes, *Directions in Sociolinguistics*, New York, Holt, Rinehart & Winston, 1972, and Jim Schenkein (ed), *Studies in the Organization of Conversational Interaction*, New York, Academic press, 1978. The 'Simplest systematics' paper by Sacks, Schegloff and Jefferson was first printed in *Language*, Vol. 50, 1974, pp. 696–735. Schegloff's paper on summons-answer pairs and conversational openings is 'Sequencing in Conversational Openings', *American Anthropologist*, 1968, Vol. 70, pp. 1075–95. An early, important, though difficult and often obscure, paper by Sacks is 'Sociological Description', *Berkeley Journal of Sociology*, 1963.

CHAPTER 6

Garfinkel has published relatively little since 1967 but a large body of his own work and that of his students has been accumulating since then, and these are now being prepared for publication in a series of books from Routledge & Kegan Paul. In the interim, the paper on the optically discovered pulsar, cited in Chapter 4, together with Michael Lynch, Eric Livingston and Harold Garfinkel, 'Temporal order in laboratory work', in Karin Knorr-Cetina and Michael Mulkay (eds), *Science Observed*, London, Sage, 1983, pp. 205–238, Michael Lynch, *Art and Artifact in Laboratory Science*, London, Routledge & Kegan Paul, 1985, and 'Discipline and the material form of images', *Social Studies of Science*, Vol. 15, 1985, pp. 37–66 and Eric Livingston, *An Ethnomethodological Investigation of the Foundation of Mathematics*, Los Angeles, Unpublished Ph.D. thesis, University of California at Los Angeles, 1983, provide some accessible sources that give a good idea of the way this work is going. The kind of study of mathematics and science with which we constrasted such studies can be found in (for example) Raymond Wilder, *Mathematics as a Cultural System*, Pergamon, 1981. Erwing Goffman's essay 'Role Distance' is in his *Encounters*, Bobbs, Merrill, Indianapolis, 1961.

CHAPTER 7

The critical appraisal of ethnomethodology covers a wide range. At one end there is the sort of *ad hominem* diatribe found in Alvin Gouldner, *The*

Coming Crisis of Western Sociology, London, Heinemann, 1970, and Ernest Gellner, 'Ethomethodology: the re-enchantment industry or the california way of subjectivity', *Philosophy of the Social Sciences*, Vol. 5, 1975, pp. 431–450. At the other end are those who are sympathetic, sensitive and yet unconvinced. Two examples of this sort are Zygmunt Bauman, *Hermeneutics and Social Science*, Hutchinson, 1978, who wishes to tackle ethnomethodology on its phenomenological credentials, and Mary Rogers, *Sociology, Ethnomethodology and Experience*, Cambridge University Press, 1983, which wants to do much the same but with less effect. Daniel O'Keefe's review of the debates is helpful and can be found in Ethnomethodology', *Journal for the Theory of Social Behaviour*, Vol. 9, 1979, pp. 187–219.

Most other critics lie somewhere in between. nearly all of them wish to point out how, if it is not to be wholly abolished, ethnomethodology would stand to be improved if it fitted more closely to their conception of what sociology ought to be about and be doing. Widely cited are Anthony Giddens, *The New Rules of Sociological Method*, London, Hutchinson, 1976, and *The Constitution of Society*, Oxford, Polity Press, and Randall Collins, *Conflict Sociology*, New York, Academic Books, 1975. There is also a selection of views in Knorr-Cetina and Cicourel (eds), *Advances in Sociological Theory and Method*, London, Routledge and Kegan Paul, 1981. The classic locale for such misunderstandings is the Review Symposium on Harold Garfinkel's *Studies in Ethnomethodology*, *American Sociological Review*, Vol. 33, 1968, pp. 122–130.

Responses from ethnomethodologists to their critics are rare. Don Zimmerman, 'Ethnomethodology' in *The American Sociologist*, Vol. 13, 1978, pp. 6–15 answers several objections, Cicourel demolishes his critics in the introduction to the second edition of his *The Social Organisation of Juvenile Justice*, London, Heinemann, 1976. A more oblique response in to be found in Egon Bittner's 'Objectivity and Realism' in George Psathas (ed), *Phenomenological Sociology*, New York, Wiley, 1973.

The call for a more fundamental re-examination of preconceptions by Blum, McHugh and their colleagues is made in, for example, Peter McHugh, Stanley Raffel, Daniel Foss and Alan Blum *On the Beginnings of Social Inquiry*, London, Routledge & Kegan Paul, 1974. The ways in which they set themselves apart from ethnomethodology can be most clearly seen in 'Snubs', Chapter 5 of that book, in which they re-examine Roy Turner's arguments in 'Words, Utterances and Activities', in Jack Douglas (ed), *Understanding Everyday Life*, London, Routledge & Kegan Paul, 1970 and in Stanley Raffel's *Masters of Fact,* Routledge & Kegan Paul, 1970, where a characteristically ethnomethodological topic, the reading of medical records, is taken in a very different direction.

Data—who needs it? by Howard Schwartz is published in *Analytic Sociology*, Vol. 2, No. 1, and the paper 'On recognizing mistakes' reprinted in Howard Schwartz and Jerry Jacobs, *Qualitative Sociology*, New York, The Free Press, 1979, pp. 405–417, can be read as an indirect criticism of conversational analysis, forgetfulness about the practices involved in hearing what utterances say. The latter part of the Schwartz/Jacobs book, i.e. Part 2, can usefully be read as a guide to some of Schwartz's general strategies.

Index